Choosing Forgiveness

John & Paula Sandford
and Lee Bowman

✤

Keys of Knowledge Series

Choosing Forgiveness

About the authors:
John and Paula Sandford are founders of Elijah House Christian Ministries, headquartered in Post Falls, Idaho. (www.elijahhouse.org) The Sandfords are veteran authors and teachers, recognized internationally as pioneers in the field of inner healing and family renewal. Their best selling books, including *The Elijah Task, The Transformation of the Inner Man*, and *Healing the Wounded Spirit*, have long been established as foundational resources for the training of Christian counselors.

Lee Bowman is president of Clear Stream Publishing in Arlington, Texas. Lee is a graduate of William Jewell College, holds a theology degree from New Orleans Baptist Theological Seminary and a masters degree in art from Vanderbilt University.

Unless otherwise noted, Scripture quotations used in this book are from the New International Version (NIV) © 1973, 1978, 1984 International Bible Society. Used by permission of Zondervan Bible Publishers. Other translations used include the New American Standard Version (NAS) and Today's English Version (TEV).

Choosing Forgiveness, Second Edition, 1999
Cover design and photography by Lee Bowman.

ISBN 0-9637741-1-5

Clear Stream, Inc. Publishing
Box 122128, Arlington, Texas 76012
www.clear-stream.com

Choosing Forgiveness

John & Paula Sandford
and Lee Bowman

Contents

About This Book

For many years now the focus of *Elijah House* has been on a ministry of restoration and reconciliation to born-again Christians who are in need of inner healing and transformation. Most of our writings and teachings have been directed toward training both professional and lay counselors to equip them to deal with the deep wounds and spiritual needs in the persons to whom they minister.

Our published works have often been used as textbooks by colleges and seminaries as they train men and women for ministry in the field of counseling and pastoral care. The comprehensive nature of these books has served that purpose well.

However, in response to numerous requests by friends and co-workers, we have undertaken a project to adapt our writings and teachings to a broader and less academic audience—to deal in more depth with specific topics and to directly address the needs of lay persons, counselees and small groups, rather than the professional counselor.

To accomplish this task, we have teamed with writer and editor Lee Bowman as co-author of a new line of books called the **Keys of Knowledge Series**. *Waking the Slumbering Spirit* was the first release in this series and *Choosing Forgiveness* is the second release.

Lee Bowman has very effectively assimilated material from our other books, lectures, tapes, schools of prayer counseling, and personal conversations—as well as contributing much material of his own—to produce an entirely new work that is exactly on target.

Choosing Forgiveness is an important work because it addresses perhaps the most universal issue everyone must deal with—learning both to give and to receive forgiveness. Unforgiveness is the root cause of practically every interpersonal relationship problem for which people come for counseling.

This book is designed for study and practical application by those seeking spiritual growth and healing which will enrich their relationships with others and with God. A study guide is included at the end of each chapter to encourage self evaluation and small group interaction.

We encourage you to use *Choosing Forgiveness* as a resource for fellowship groups, Sunday School classes, home Bible studies, and discipleship training groups. Please contact us through Elijah House or Clear Stream Publishing with your feedback.

John & Paula Sandford

Prelude
Navigating the Stream of Life
by Lee Bowman

So much to think about! So many to forgive! The morning air was crisp and clean as the blanket of mist began to lift slowly from the valley floor. Long shafts of sunlight broke through puffy white clouds floating along the horizon, sending sparkling rays of yellow light dancing across the green Middle Tennessee meadows. The birds were singing. The gentle breeze rustled softly through the treetops. Everything seemed at peace except for the battle raging in my head.

I had come for a weekend retreat in the country, seeking counsel from Christian friends in hopes of working through some of the anguish that had been burdening me for months. I felt overcome with betrayal, anger, and bitterness. My marriage on the rocks, career jeopardized, separation from my children threatened, alienated from old friends, in financial crisis, and floating in moral ambiguity—I was in a state of unbearable turmoil.

Our group session the night before had been difficult but productive, with lots of "stuff" uncovered and true feelings exposed. I thought I was ripe for some resolution and was looking forward to more self disclosure with my group. But that morning our leader assigned us an exercise in silence. He said we were to spend the morning "alone and in personal reflection, experiencing nature and discovering what could be learned from a time of quiet contemplation."

My mind was neither quiet nor contemplative as I reluctantly headed down a path toward the open fields and the woods beyond. I had come for comfort and counsel and was being asked to experience more loneliness and silence. I felt depressed, angry, and confused.

   In frustration, I began to jog down the path in a blind attempt to flee my own tumultuous feelings. As I reached the edge of the open field, I picked up the pace and broke into a full run. Running felt good—my legs stretching out over the rough ground, feet pounding into the moist soil, the cool morning air against my face. I ran freely across the softly rolling pastureland, becoming incredibly aware of the open expanse of sky above and the sweet smell of the earth beneath my feet.

I ran and I ran, my body sometimes straining to go faster than my weary legs would allow. Stumbling from time to time over the rough terrain, I desperately struggled to retain my balance and push on. Near exhaustion, I finally reached the narrow strip of woods that ran like a ribbon along the creek below the rolling fields. Gasping for breath and with lungs burning, I stretched out face down on the trunk of a large fallen tree that lay across the stream.

I lay there on the log for a long time with eyes closed and the morning sun warm against my back. Finally, when the sound of my pounding heart subsided enough to hear the soft gurgling of the stream below, I opened my eyes and gazed down into the water.

Immediately below me, the stream ran deep and swift with clear, sparkling current cutting a channel down the center of the creek bed. Large stones lined the bottom, worn smooth by the ever-rushing water. The stones were slick and shining in the reflected light of the morning sun.

On each side of the creek, closer to the bank, the water drifted by more slowly across a shallow bed of fine gravel. The smooth surface of the stream was broken randomly by partially submerged branches, drifting leaves, and other floating debris.

Across the creek in a low and muddy backwash area, the shallow water lay perfectly still, brown with algae and silt and topped with a layer of scum.

In quiet reverie I studied the stream and began to see a world completely within itself. A dozen minnows came swimming into view. Some launched out into the center of the stream where the water ran clear and swift. Playing in the current, they darted by like tiny silver flashes of light. Others, attempting to swim upstream fought the current, barely able to make headway. They wriggled furiously to reach their goal.

Still other minnows seemed to prefer the shallows along the bank. They floated lazily in the quiet water as though happy to be in safe harbor, out of the turbulent current. A larger fish came swimming by and the minnows, reacting in fright, darted quickly for protection beneath a sunken log until the danger passed.

Fish would not swim in the shallow pools of brackish backwater. Muddy and stagnant, those pools lay quietly and passively evaporating in the sun. One small fish lay dead, apparently trapped in the shallow pool when high water had receded. It floated on the surface, surrounded by algae and foam.

That quiet morning alone in nature proved to be a turning point in life for me. As I lay prone on a fallen log above an ever-flowing stream, the world I observed crystallized a clear message presented by God for me to understand.

What course would I follow?
- ◆ Would I be caught in stagnant waters, feeling hopelessly trapped while life-giving nourishment slowly evaporates around me?
- ◆ Would I be content to wait in quiet shallowness, hoping to be left alone, unchallenged?
- ◆ When threatened, would I flee in fear to the safety of another hiding place?
- ◆ Would I spend myself in furious swimming against the current, helplessly awash in the swift stream of life, and fighting against it all the way?
- ◆ Or, would I be one to choose where I swim—sometimes feeding in the quiet harbor of a peaceful pool, sometimes valiantly fighting the torrent to survive, sometimes choosing to let go with happy abandon as the clear current sweeps downstream to a new adventure and a new day?

   The stream of life continues to flow today, and we are all inextricably a part of it. How will we respond and where will we swim? Will we be helpless victims living in bitterness and self-doubt, or proactive affirmers of life, willing to forgive and to bless those who would harm us?

> *Each moment is mine!*
> *No matter what my journey has been;*
> *No matter what nurturing or lack of nurturing*
> *I have experienced;*
> *No matter what pain and scars I bear—*
> *From this moment on,*
> *Life is a choosing.*

Chapter One

Forgiveness: Option or Necessity?

Choosing to Journey Toward the Light

Painful confrontations
Become fears
From which I
*   R E C O I L —*
The stimulus lodged in memories
Which wound with each recall.

Anger thrown against the wind
Sends echoes bouncing back again,
And here I stand alone
Shouting down the memories
Of the many times I've failed—
Hurting through it all
But unyielding to the fear.

What is despair
But dying to the hope inside?
Fear has not conquered—
For the hope still lives.
The more I risk
The more I win.
I must canonize that lesson
Again and again
And again.

Lee Bowman

What significance is there to our living if we do not learn important lessons from our mistakes—and discover ways to keep from repeating errors which chain us to unhappy and unproductive ways? After all, life is a choosing!

❧ *Lee*

Even in the heat of my anger, there was that split second to decide whether to hit him. I was about twelve years old and I had irritated my friend John Livengood enough to make him really angry. He called me a dirty name which served to get me heated up too. I stood there with clinched fists for that emotionally charged instant, then chose to add injury to insult by taking a hefty swing at his face.

My fist missed his chin and landed squarely on his Adam's apple! He fell to his knees, writhing in pain and gasping for breath. The blow did no real damage, except to his feelings, because as soon as he was able to talk, he proceeded to curse me further and accuse me of fighting dirty. He was sure I meant to hit him in the throat—and would forever hold it against me.

As I recall, I wasn't sorry I hurt him, but I did regret missing my target. Yet I was not about to apologize as long as he had such a rotten attitude. He said I started the fight, but I knew that he had—and we never wanted to be close friends after that.

Years later, reflecting on my fight with John Livengood, I realized we were but a microcosm of the way most of the world behaves. We simply chose to sin against each other and then to live in unforgiveness.

The law of sowing and reaping.

Sin and unforgiveness are not happy issues to think about and most of us characteristically avoid dealing with them if we can get away with it. Ego and pride are involved when we have been hurt by someone—and in the eyes of the world, it seems natural for someone who has been hurt to seek revenge. But our sin and unforgiveness have a way of rebounding and keeping us constantly in trouble. Sin is what isolates us from God, from one another, and from our own self. Unforgiveness preserves and calcifies the isolation and keeps us from seeking reconciliation and achieving wholeness.

Forgiveness is the antidote to sin. Forgiveness reunites us with God, brings us into unity with one another, and restores the integrity of our inner self. That is why forgiveness is central to all of life. If we are to be happy, healthy, and grow in relationships with others, forgiveness is not an option, it is a necessity.

Forgiveness is the most important and joyous message the Gospel of the Lord Jesus Christ brings to us.

God gives us ability to make choices, but we must live with the results of our choosing. We can be stuck with unforgiveness forever and be miserable, or we can choose to forgive and enjoy the benefits of freedom it brings. If we have always thought forgiving or not forgiving was just a matter of personal choice, depending on the intensity of our feelings, we need to consider how the Scriptures command us to forgive:

> *For if you forgive men when they sin against you, your heavenly Father will also forgive you. But if you do not forgive men their sins, your Father will not forgive your sins.*
> *(Matthew 6:14-15)*

Why does Jesus express this so strongly, so absolutely? God created an orderly universe based on natural laws or principles. Just as we know that certain laws of physics are unalterably true and predictable, so we should understand that God has spiritual laws which are true and predictable. Wouldn't it be silly if our legislators got together and decided to repeal the law of gravity? They could unanimously vote gravity out of existence—but it would make absolutely no difference in the way planets revolve around the sun or the way we are held to the earth and kept from being flung out into space by the centrifugal force of the earth's rotation.

The reality of a parallel realm of immutable spiritual laws is rejected by many people today who would prefer to base ethical behavior on relative values left to each person's interpretation. History alone should demonstrate to us that principles such as those spelled out in the Ten Commandments God gave to Moses are essential foundation stones for human behavior. As famous movie director Cecil B. deMille is reported to have said while making the movie *The Ten Commandments*, "It is impossible for us to break the law. We can only break ourselves against the law."

Stephen Covey, author of the immensely influential book *The 7 Habits of Highly Effective People*, speaks directly to the issue of immutable principles that govern human relationships and happiness. Covey says: *"I believe that correct principles are natural laws, and that God, the Creator and Father of us all, is the source of them, and also the source of our conscience. I believe that to the degree people live by this inspired conscience, they will grow to fulfill their natures; to the degree that they do not, they will not rise above the animal plane."*[1]

We need to recognize how the universe works.
We will reap what we sow!

The principle of sowing and reaping is one of God's absolute laws. If we sow judgment, we will reap judgment. If we sow blessing, we will reap blessing. If we sow unforgiveness, we will reap the same. It is not God's intention to punish us by this standard. Rather, He loves us so much that He wants us to understand how His universe works so we don't have to reap unaware.

The consequences of breaking God's laws are fixed. The choice is ours to receive blessing or reject it.

And when you stand praying, if you hold anything against anyone, forgive him, so that your Father in heaven may forgive you your sins. (Mark 11:25-26)

So watch yourselves. If your brother sins, rebuke him, and if he repents, forgive him. If he sins against you seven times in a day, and seven times comes back to you and says "I repent," forgive him. (Luke 17:3-4)

Be kind and compassionate to one another, forgiving each other, just as in Christ God forgave you. *(Ephesians 4:32)*

Therefore, as God's chosen people, holy and dearly loved, clothe yourselves with compassion, kindness, humility, gentleness, and patience. Bear with each other and forgive whatever grievances you may have against one another. Forgive as the Lord forgave you. *(Colossians 3:12-13)*

What does love have to do with forgiveness?

The process of forgiveness must begin with a simple act of choosing to begin the journey of forgiveness. Many people are reluctant to take that first step of choosing to forgive, believing that if they follow the path of forgiveness they will become weaklings who are consistently taken advantage of by others. This is not what forgiveness, grounded in love, is about. True love encourages a compassionate willingness to forgive, yet retains the strength of conviction that all parties must be fully accountable for their own decisions and behavior.

Forgiveness grounded in true love is not a soft and naive yielding that excuses almost any kind of abuse people might direct at us. It is not a self-effacing meekness that lets people run all over us. True love releases a power within that enables us to make that risky decision to choose to forgive and to deal with the dynamics of working through what can be a painful give-and-take experience.

A teacher of the law once asked Jesus what the most important commandment was. Jesus replied:

Love the Lord your God with all your heart and with all your soul and with all your mind and with all your strength. The second is this: Love your neighbor as yourself. There is no commandment greater than these. *(Mark 12:30-31)*

If we love our neighbor rightly, the implication of Jesus' command is that we must also love ourselves. Loving ourselves doesn't mean selfishly looking out for our own interests at the expense of others. It means caring for and seeking the healthiest possible nurture for ourselves and being concerned for the well-being of others to the same degree. Healthy self-love hinges on self-respect and we must guard against excusing any behavior or attitude in others that will undermine our personal integrity or jeopardize theirs. Respecting self requires that we discern appropriate boundaries and set limits to the amount of mistreatment we will accept from those who are thoughtless or who would be cruel.

Healthy expressions of love will not permit the shouldering of blame for the wrongs others commit or the stoic toleration of destructive behavior on the assumption they can't help themselves. We must be willing to forgive, but we must also know where to draw lines of accountability. In the name of love, we do not have to passively accept disloyalty from trusted friends, betrayal from our spouse, abuse from our family members, or the deceit of professional co-workers. That is not what forgiveness is. True love should empower us to say "No more!" when someone's behavior pushes past our boundaries. We must expect each person to be accountable for his or her actions—and that includes ourself.

This is a strong message for those caught in co-dependent relationships in which they tolerate, compensate for, or excuse dysfunctional lifestyles of loved ones and thereby enable them to continue to wound the lives of others. Love and forgiveness should not shield even those we love the most from the consequences of their decisions.

Love and accountability.
Love is compassionate, but it is also strong. Love is strong because it is God's way and when we love in God's name, we act in the enabling power of His Holy Spirit. Such love is grounded in the authority of God and commands respect. It allows us to relate to others with integrity and enables us to take the risk of seeking committed relationships. Those who lack this divinely inspired power of love are more likely to fear commitment and less likely to risk forgiving others.

To show true love toward others is to respect them enough to allow them to be accountable, particularly for the wounds they inflict on other people. *Letting* persons be accountable is different than *demanding* they be accountable. We cannot demand another persons repentance, and we seldom can establish a level of consequence that represents justice for their infractions. Even if we could control others by our demands, we would be robbing them of their personhood by making their decisions for them.

Letting persons be accountable means respecting their personhood by allowing them to experience whatever the consequences are for their actions. Outside of the requirements of criminal law, we should neither protectively excuse nor vindictively punish other persons for the way they have hurt us. To do so is to usurp their own accountability and thus to show them disrespect.

Forgiveness is not the same as pardoning. To pardon is to end all judgment, to lift away all due reaping for sowing. God may pardon if He so chooses. We are called and given the authority only to forgive.

Expressing love inevitably pushes us to crises of decision:

- ♦ Do we forever hold on to the hurt, nurturing our pain and feeling it again and again with each remembrance? Or, will the power of our self-respecting love reverse the tide of our feelings?

- ♦ Is our willingness to be forgiving contingent on the offender's repentant attitude? Or, can we choose to forgive regardless of how the offender may respond?

Simply speaking, can we choose to love our enemies and be kind to those who hatefully use us? Real love respects people even in the midst of their human frailties. When love restores one's self-respect by drawing clear lines of tolerance and honestly placing accountability where it belongs, forgiveness becomes more of a possibility. We can shift the focus of our attention from ourselves and begin to point our love toward those who have hurt us. Our willingness to respect others allows us to take that first step of choosing to forgive and enables us to move on to the healing of hurts which can be accomplished through the power of God's Holy Spirit.

The enabling power of the Lord Jesus Christ.

We know the Son of God by many names: Jesus, Lord, Redeemer, Light, Messiah, Truth, Christ, the Word. For the purpose of gaining insight into the absolute necessity of forgiveness, we need to understand the meaning of the title most often used in the New Testament. That title is **Lord Jesus Christ.**

It is interesting to note how many times in the New Testament the disciples called Jesus by this full title of the three names. For example, Paul began his letter to the church at Thessalonica in this way:

> *To the church of the Thessalonians in God the Father and the* ***Lord Jesus Christ****: Grace and peace to you. We always thank God for all of you, mentioning you in our prayers. We continually remember before our God and Father your work produced by faith, your labor prompted by love, and your endurance inspired by hope in our* ***Lord Jesus Christ****.*
>
>

(1 Thessalonians 1:1-3)

Use of this title is not just a verbal issue. His title represents three basic aspects of the authority Jesus has in establishing the Kingdom of God.

♦Because Jesus is *Lord,* He can accomplish forgiveness. The Pharisees, who doubted Him, asked: *"What manner of man is this that He even forgives sins?"* He can forgive sins because He is the Lord of the universe. He has authority over all things and through His power accomplishes forgiveness where man cannot.

♦Because Christ the Lord is *Jesus,* the Son of Man, He became the sacrifice necessary to accomplish forgiveness. Although He was the Son of God, He was also fully man, who suffered, died on the cross, and was buried, taking the full weight of mankind's sin upon Himself. He conquered death by rising from the grave, providing salvation and eternal life for those who believe in Him as their Savior.

♦Because Jesus is *Christ,* the anointed one of God, He became the perfect sacrifice to provide salvation from sin and to make a way for forgiveness. As Christ the Savior, Jesus brings reconciliation between man and God, between man and man, between man and his own inner being, and even between man and nature.

Many people believe Jesus was simply a wise and godly teacher who lived and died two thousand years ago. They don't understand or believe that Jesus is the Son of God—that He rose from the dead, conquering sin and death on behalf of all men and women, and that through faith in Him we share that victory. They don't understand that to receive Christ as Savior means that the living Christ comes to live in us, and we are to live in Him. Consequently, they think salvation is up to themselves.

> ### *It is Jesus Christ*
> ### *who makes forgiveness possible,*
> ### *because it is He*
> ### *who conquered sin and death.*

Those who struggle with forgiveness may say: *"I have tried and tried to forgive, but I just can't seem to get it done."* If we think it is up to us to accomplish forgiveness through our striving, we will never *"get it done."* We must understand that forgiveness comes through what the Lord Jesus Christ has *already* accomplished. He has taken that burden from us and through His grace we can forgive, even when by the standards of our human emotion it seems virtually impossible.

If we want to claim the richness and freedom of relationship with God and with others that comes with being forgiven of our sins by our Heavenly Father, we must seek to forgive others of the sins they commit against us. But forgiveness is not as simple or as easy as just making a choice to forgive. It may take years of our disciplined commitment to the task before we allow the grace of God to fully penetrate our hardened hearts and produce the desired good fruit in our lives.

Subsequent chapters will deal in more depth with how the process of forgiveness can be played out in our lives.

[1.] Stephen R. Covey, *The 7 Habits of Highly Effective People,* Fireside, Simon & Schuster, New York, NY, © 1989 by Stephen Covey

Lord of the Universe, Maker of Heaven and Earth, Author of All Life, Righteous Loving Father,

Thank You for Your wisdom in giving us the unchangeable laws of nature and the immutable spiritual principles which govern human behavior.

Help me to realize that I will reap what I sow and that the path of unforgiveness in my life will lead to destruction and isolation from You and from others. Forgive me when I rebel against Your shepherding and seek my selfish will over Your loving provision.

I ask for strength to bear up under my woundings, the grace to choose to forgive, the wisdom to allow others to be accountable for their actions, and the courage to repentantly confess my own sins.

Help me to see that I do not have to accomplish forgiveness on my own—that You are my loving Father who is there to bring me into refreshing new relationships through the power of what the Lord Jesus Christ did for me on the cross.

Amen

Life Application:
Forgiveness: Option or Necessity?

The following chart provides an opportunity for you to map out where you are with some personal unforgivenesses in your life. Read the instructions and complete each column as honestly as you can.

A. In column A, make a list of people toward whom you feel some degree of unforgiveness in each category.

Offenses for which we judge others in unforgiveness	**A.** Person toward whom you feel unforgiving	**B.** Have you clearly defined your boundaries?	**C.** Has account-ability been established?	**D.** Are you willing to choose to forgive?
Disloyalty from a friend				
Betrayal from a spouse/relative				
Abuse from a family member				
Deceit of a co-worker				
Hurt from a stranger/group				

B. Consider how well-equipped you are to deal with each of these unforgivenesses listed above. Have you clearly defined the boundaries of what you are willing to tolerate from the situation? For each issue above, place a *Yes* or *No* in the box in column B. If you answered *Yes*, write out below a clear statement of your position, considering what you must do to protect yourself against further abuse without being vindictive toward the other person.

    To avoid my continuing to be hurt, I must:

C. All of us must bear responsibility for ways in which we contribute to broken relationships or hurtful situations. However, one cannot assume responsibility for another person's attitude or behavior. Do you clearly understand how this person who hurt you must personally be accountable for his/her actions? For each issue above, place a *Yes* or *No* in the box in column C. If you have been unwisely assuming responsibility for other people, how can you withdraw from assuming that burden?

D. Are you willing to begin the process of forgiving the persons who hurt you, no matter what their response might be? For each issue above, place a *Yes* or *No* in the box in column D.

Share your responses above with a friend or with your group members. Choose one of the situations you face and define the positive and negative aspects of being forgiving in that particular situation. Consider the law of sowing and reaping and then write your thoughts below.

What will I reap if I choose to forgive?

What will I reap if I don't choose to forgive?

Discuss with a friend or with your group the concept of how the Lord Jesus Christ can achieve forgiveness in you even when you don't seem to be able to accomplish it by your own will.

Read again the prayer on page 20 and apply it to a specific situation in your life in which you are choosing forgiveness.

Chapter Two

The Pigpen Dilemma
Making Personal Peace in an Unjust World

Thank you loving Father
That my striving now can end.
You have tucked my crimson edge of living
Behind the golden sun of new beginnings,
Defining where I'm going
From where I've been.

Streams of light rip through
The darkness of my void
In magnificent diffusion—
The afterglow of images
Still remembered but no longer feared.
Grieving eyes that searched so frantically
For lost innocence
Are now innocently discovering
New landscapes—
Rich, but yet unmined.

Visions of revisions
Rewind of time.
If it wasn't for the old songs
New songs wouldn't rhyme.

Lee Bowman

Eager to be free from his family and out on his own, a young man took his inheritance and traveled to a distant land where he soon squandered with foolish living all that he had. Falling into severe need, he hired himself out for what he could get—feeding pigs in the fields and eating that which was intended only for animals. Coming to his senses, he longingly wished for his home. He determined to return to his father, make amends for his sinful behavior, and seek forgiveness from his family . . .

(Paraphrased from Luke 15)

When teaching about forgiveness, we often sense some in the audience reacting to the idea that giving or receiving forgiveness might require rigorous personal discipline. They want forgiveness to be easy. They don't want to be told that getting into position to receive the grace of forgiveness will require working daily at the discipline of forgiving others. They don't want to be told they must go through the effort of constantly blessing those who hurt them. Yes, it would be nice if the heart would always just flop to the flip side of good feelings once the grace of Jesus is invited. The fact is, forgiveness seldom comes that easily.

Forgiveness tested.
We can testify to a time in our lives when it seemed the Lord said, *"Okay, John and Paula, you've been teaching this for twenty years, now let's see if you can live it!"* We got hit with five major blows—betrayals, attacks—all at the same time:

1. A popular book debunked what we taught, told lies many believed about us and our teaching, and brought us into disrepute.

2. Our son-in-law sexually abused our granddaughter.

3. A colleague and friend on our counseling staff was discovered to be using his position to seduce women.

4. Our then publisher stopped paying any of his writers their royalties, and we lost many thousands of dollars we had counted on for the tuition and expenses of our sons in college and seminary.

5. The denomination in which we had spent our entire life and ministry became so apostate we had to leave it.

All five of these events hurt terribly—any one by itself would have been enough to crush our hearts in grief. We had to take hold of our thoughts and emotions and make ourselves practice what we had taught! The joy in the midst of pain for us was to learn that God is indeed faithful to heal.

Sometimes He heals easily and quickly just because it's His nature to love us and want to comfort. But sometimes, in His wisdom, He knows shortcuts won't be good for us; we'll have to take the long road of struggle and discipline, making ourselves obey when everything in us cries out to go the other way. In all these situations, we proactively chose to forgive and to seek ways to express ourselves in love:

1. Despite the pain of being misunderstood, misrepresented, and having our ministry damaged by published false accusations, we ultimately chose to pray blessing for the man who was our detractor. The result has been a wonderful healing within our own hearts. We also have witnessed a growing vindication for our teachings on inner healing and for the entire ministry in which we are involved.

2. The sexual abuse of our granddaughter produced a broken marriage, years of trauma and stress for our granddaughter, our daughter, and the rest of the family—and a prison term for our son-in-law. During his prison term, he was allowed release time for two hours each Sunday to come into the fellowship and nurture of our church. Due to his repentance and working through of the process of forgiveness, a healing and renewal in the lives of everyone involved is well underway.

3. Our friend and colleague in the ministry lost his credibility, his counseling career, and his family as a result of his sin. However, forgiveness has kept open a channel of communication and love for each of us. With our blessing, he has sought to rebuild his life in a new career.

4. We and several other Christian writers who had been cheated out of royalties by our previous publisher chose to take our losses rather than to further damage the Body of Christ by becoming involved in civil litigation. Now, after many years, it appears that new management of that publishing company is interested in seeking to redress those wrongs by proposing a settlement with us. We leave that issue to be properly resolved through the grace of God.

5. We are mindful that the leadership of any denomination is vulnerable to apostasy. History is replete with stories of those who have fallen away from the high calling of God's Word. Giving up friendships and loyalty to a denomination in which we served so long was disappointing and painful, but the Lord's work is not bound by denominationalism. Although we can no longer in good conscience serve under the authority of those who governed us in our pastoral ministry, we hold no bitterness. The Lord is the head of all Christian churches and His Spirit moves mightily among those individuals who remain faithful, no matter where they serve.

The thesis of this book is to say that when unforgiveness has lodged deeply in the heart, most often there will be no easy solution. We will have to "work out our salvation with fear and trembling," making ourselves get into Gethsemane, declaring forgiveness, and then not allowing ourselves the luxury of slacking off. We must come to realize, like an alcoholic in AA, if we don't keep on "working our program," making ourselves bless until our heart comes right again, we won't arrive at wholeness and freedom.

At times, when we teach, we can "hear" the hearts of some saying, *"It's too tough. I hear you testifying it worked for you, but how do I know it will work for me? You haven't been through the tough times I have. I didn't have just five blows, my life has been nothing but blows!"* We've heard incredible stories of betrayals that went on for years—rapes, molestations, divorces, and brutalities. These realities have made us think, *"Oh God, how grateful we ought to be! We've not had to suffer anything like these people. How could we blame them for doubting whether the disciplines of forgiveness could work for them?"*

For that reason, we are thankful that we can include the testimony of two friends and colleagues, **Charlie Finck** and **Howard**

Olsen. They are living illustrations of how the Lord can be faithful to those who seek Him over the long haul, how He heals deep wounds and transforms lives, and how He brings lost children back into relationship to serve meaningfully and joyfully in the Kingdom of God.

Charlie Finck is one of our staff counselors at *Elijah House* in Post Falls, Idaho. His story is that of a young man who was lost to his own identity, devoid of feeling loved, and wandering for many years in a far country—searching in the emptiness of sex and alcohol for fulfillment that he could not grasp by his own striving. A solid education and career as an Air Force pilot did not save him from two broken marriages and the nagging pain of deeply suppressed anger and unforgiveness. Yet Charlie persevered. He learned to listen to God and to obey. The result has been a long and difficult thirty-five year journey of inner healing and transformation that is now resulting in ever-increasing joy and fulfillment. In his own words, here is Charlie's story.

Charlie Finck

It was a scorching summer day and I had just completed a ten-mile training run in preparation for a race in the fall. I had pushed hard and was hot and tired. As I relaxed in the shower, the cascade of cool water over my body felt wonderful. My mind and my body had just begun to relax and enjoy, when suddenly a surprising thought popped into my mind.

"I want you to love your father."

At that time in my life I was making a real effort to be sensitive to the ways in which God communicates His will, and there was no doubt in my mind where that thought came from. The Lord was raising an issue that I had been very reluctant to deal with, and I instantly began to defend myself. I'd spent thirty-five years hating my father and now I was supposed to love him?

"But he's supposed to love me!" my mind screamed out to God. *"Shouldn't a father be the one to love his son?"*

Memories flooded my mind. I recalled the time as a six-year-old when I was observed putting too much salt on my food and my Dad angrily overturned my plate of food on the table and chased me around the house. I remembered the fights Dad picked with me just before my birthdays, which he was then able to ignore. The cold sullen anger I sensed from him set off a bitterness in me that became deeply lodged in my heart. I had often asked myself, *"Do I have any value to him? Any value at all?"*

My perception as a boy was that Dad not only didn't love me but was constantly annoyed by my presence. I recall approaching him as he relaxed in his favorite chair—the image of a stern and impatient king, seated on a maroon velvet throne. I always sensed his irritation even before I spoke. Whatever was on television must have been much more important. When I finally risked speaking, he would turn with a disgusted look, rubbing the back of his neck as if to remove something caustic, and say angrily, "What?"

I learned early in life not to approach Dad for anything and eventually to ignore him altogether. Focusing on relating to my mother and two sisters, Peggy and Penny, I insulated myself from my father. At the time it seemed like the safest and best way to live, although it was not without much pain and guilt. I wanted more out of my relationship with Dad, but it seemed impossible, so my frustration and anger were shoved deep down inside me.

Facts aren't judgments.

Now as I recall these experiences, I feel some discomfort about sharing them. However, I know my discomfort is false guilt. As a counselor for many years at Elijah House, I have encouraged people to share the truth about their lives. Facts aren't judgments, and sharing truth is not disloyalty.

But I did as do many of those I counsel—I held the truth in for years, along with the anger, rage, and hate. I hid my feelings away in false hope that if I didn't talk about my hate, it wouldn't really exist. I also feared that if I shared my feelings with my sisters, I might learn that their perceptions of "truth" were different than mine, thus separating me even more from my family.

When I left home to go away to college, I found myself swallowed up in the strange paradox of being free from the oppressive restrictions and dysfunctional relationships I had with my parents, but totally incapable of monitoring my own behavior since I knew so little of who I really was. As a result, in the loose moral structures of college life in the 1960s, I discovered alcohol and sex and became extremely infatuated with both.

Drinking seemed to be such fun because until then I never realized that I could feel so good. It provided a welcome relief from everything that had been building up inside me. Previously I had developed no real experience of relating to girls, but when I took a few drinks, I could relate to girls very well. I soon learned to depend on drinking to relate to others. The sex was casual, the drinking was without thought of consequences, and I became addicted to both. Until I stopped drinking years later, I never realized what a donkey people make of themselves through alcohol.

My mother played a big part in my life, and I think it was her faithful prayers that helped me through the worst of those years in which I was floundering. However, I learned over time the extent to which my mother had contributed to some of my woundings by thrusting me into parental inversion and making me a substitute mate. In counseling after a second failed marriage, I listened with anger and disbelief when I heard the words, *"Charlie, you hate your mother.*" I thought it was only my father I hated, surely not Mom. Clearly, I felt the consequences of my mother's mistakes, but in the closeness of our relationship, I never actually allowed myself to feel the hate.

In counseling, I began to acknowledge the years of my disrespect for God, Dad, Mom, and myself. I came to acknowledge the twenty years of erratic behavior brought on by drinking; the sexual addiction that took the place of intimacy; the destructive behavior that almost killed me several times and dealt near death blows to my spirit; and the relationships which seemed so necessary but which were in fact paralyzing.

In the midst of all this, the concept of accomplishing forgiveness was foreign to me. I'd love to be able to say that as a result of counseling, healing, and the Lord's presence in my life, there was instant change. But that isn't so. As I learned what it meant to forgive, especially to forgive my Dad and Mom and myself, my life gradually changed.

I want you to love your father.

Standing in the shower that summer day, I anguished and debated with God, wondering what kind of ironic sense of humor would make Him command me to love my father. But deep down, I knew it would be the key to my healing and my survival.

I made the decision that day to love and forgive. I didn't have any idea how to begin, but I knew I would try to love my father. I wanted to tell him that I loved him. It wasn't the truth, but I believed if I said the words, my heart would follow. Within an hour, I called him in New Jersey, and after a brief conversation, I said to him, *"I love you, Dad."*

Somehow it seemed easy, maybe because I didn't really mean it. He ignored my words, but that didn't matter either. I had begun. Not long after that I began to take what I had learned about forgiveness and put it into practice.

> *"Lord, I forgive my Dad. Take the bitterness and judgment out of my heart. It has almost killed me, Lord, and I don't want it there any more. I surrender it to You and ask You to remove it, to heal me where I have been wounded. Lord, I choose not to*

blame my Dad or hold his actions against him. I give up my right to be paid back for my loss by the one who has sinned against me—and in so doing, I declare my trust in You alone as my righteous judge."

As I examined these words I had learned to pray, I realized I had never really forgiven anyone or anything in my life. I had gone through the motions, saying the words *"I forgive you"* when it seemed appropriate, but never really choosing to let go of the judgment and debt. When I honestly began to let go of the judgment, the healing began, and I've spent many of the years since in sheer repetition—forgiving my father and mother and the many others I perceived as hurting me, recognizing that every time I experienced hurt, whether real or perceived, I had blamed and judged. At times, my anger and bitterness went so deep even seventy times seven forgivenesses didn't seem enough.

> **I had to continually remind myself**
> **that the Lord had a work to do in me,**
> **and I had to clear the way by choosing to forgive.**

Since that time when I honestly began letting go of my judgments, the Lord has truly changed my life. Through a sovereign act of God, He caused me to see the negative force of alcohol abuse on my behavior. I was able to stop drinking immediately and have never taken a drop since. The Lord brought Deborah into my life as a wonderful marriage partner, and He has blessed us with the precious gift of an adopted son, Jonathan. My years of counseling and teaching at Elijah House have given me the privilege of sharing God's healing and grace with thousands of people.

I don't mean to say that all change in my life came from just forgiveness, but the alcohol, the sexual addiction, the hate, and the rage that permeated my life were all a part of my unforgiveness. As I chose to forgive, not by what I felt, but by an act of will, I opened the door to God's restoration in my life.

A few years ago when my father was eighty-two years old and no longer able to manage living on his own, we invited him to come live with us. It seemed a miracle to me that I was able to make such an offer. The Lord brought compassion and love where there had once been hate and anger. Deborah and I hoped to share our love and the Lord's with my father. But the years had done little to change Dad, and it wasn't easy for him to be a member of a family. Despite our good efforts, his anger and dissatisfaction filled our home and occupied most of our lives. It seemed especially difficult for Deborah, who had given up her teaching position to stay home and care for him. Nonetheless, we had hoped for more—that Dad could find some of the Lord's peace and joy in our home. The happiest solution for us all was for my Dad to move into a lovely retirement facility close by where he could live as independently as he had for the seventeen years since my mother's death.

It was difficult to see him go, although we agreed it was best for all of us. Only a few days after Dad had settled into his new apartment, a friend called offering us the opportunity to adopt Jonathan. Later, as I walked through the hallway past Dad's empty bedroom, I wondered if God perhaps had just made a place for the child we wanted so much. Our home seemed peaceful again—a good place for a boy to grow.

My father lives a troubled life. At eighty-four, he finds himself wondering what he might have done differently. He doesn't like growing old. But I can now truthfully say I love him, and lately we've been having some very good times together, laughing and talking about his life. God's wisdom and His grace abound!

Howard Olsen's story illustrates the common striving of many of us—burdened with unforgivenesses lodged in our hearts, unable to make sense of an unjust and cruel world, feeling we have no place to belong, caught up in deeply wounding events over which we have had no control, and struggling to identify who and what it is we need to forgive in order to be healed.

What could have been more devastating to a generation of young people than to be involved in the merciless horrors of the Vietnam war, and then come home to the betrayal of rejection suffered from the very Americans they had been laying down their lives to serve? Howard tells his story with brutal self-honesty, revealing the depths of his torn heart, so that we might see, however bad our personal history might be, God *can* heal us—if we will let Him.

Howard Olsen lives in Fort Worth, Texas, with his wife Myrna and youngest son Brady. He is a mature and committed Christian, investing himself in a faith ministry as a Christian counselor and seminar leader and in a continuing ministry of support among Vietnam veterans who suffer from post-traumatic stress disorder. His book *Wounded Warriors, Chosen Lives* is published by Clear Stream Publishing. In his own words, here is Howard's story.

Howard Olsen

Tell me if I'm wrong. But I think everyone, at some stage of life, experiences feelings of general unrest and confusion that seize the soul. I have experienced such feelings, and they have been a constant emotional theme with many people I have counseled over the years.

We may be aware when something is hindering our relationships with others, but we don't know what it is. Something stands in the way of our experiencing genuine intimacy with God, but we can't identify it. We sense there's more to life than what we are experiencing, but we don't know what is lacking. The relationships we have, or the work we do, leave us somehow unfulfilled. We might sense our unrest is connected to dissatisfaction with relationships, but we don't know how to work through it.

General feelings of unrest, mistrust, fear, anxiety, or anger always have specific origins. As adults we may be far removed from the childhood or adolescent experiences which firmly set emotional, mental, or behavioral patterns in our life. We've forgotten them. Consequently, we are unable to identify their origin.

While experiences from our distant past may not appear particularly important or traumatic to us as adults, they may have dramatically shaped our world-view as children. As adults, we tend to justify, excuse, or rationalize our past, but we may never deal with the underlying emotional baggage we carry.

In adult life we may also have painful and traumatic experiences which result in life-changing beliefs, behaviors, and emotional patterns. If we do not constantly resolve experiences which deeply wound us, we must carry those feelings as baggage as well.

As we progress through life, our experiences may confirm conclusions we reached as children or in our formative adolescent years. Beliefs, emotional responses, and fixed patterns of behavior begin to generalize. They slowly escalate, become more widespread or encompassing, and affect the way we relate to others or to similar situations. In turn, these same beliefs or fixed ways of perceiving life tend to constrict or restrict our activities.

We can eventually reach a stage in life in which we live in confusion. Our feelings and motives may become murky and obscure. We can't describe how we feel, and we're not sure what we want. It is as though we're groping through an emotional mist, unable to determine how we got lost or how to find our way out. We may feel imprisoned by overwhelming or lingering emotions over which it seems we have no control.

Thank God that even though we may not be able "to see the forest through the trees," through His grace we can be set in heavenly places. In Jesus Christ, we can be raised to a higher and clearer vantage point. He can enable us to see where the forest begins and ends, and He can walk with us to find the way out.

In the summer of 1967 I found myself wandering on the West Coast, alienated from my parents and isolated from an expanding segment of American society. Although I was only nineteen years old, increasing periods of loneliness and despair were driving me into an alcoholic lifestyle. Depression was slowly becoming a chronic nightmare that often slipped up on me unaware. Bleak, sullen, cheerless periods of intense darkness accompanied my drinking. In the middle of such despondency I could not be approached without setting off a stream of ugly, piercing, hateful words that hurt those who tried to penetrate my barrier of misery.

Yearning for love but fearing rejection.
I trusted very few people and could be vulnerable to no one. I felt trapped by emotions I had no control over—feelings that seemed to engulf my life without reason or rhyme. I would not acknowledge my feelings because I saw them as weaknesses. To admit I had weaknesses was to admit I had needs that could make me vulnerable.

A part of me longed to understand what I was going through. I began a careful search for answers. I quit talking to nearly everyone. I withdrew into passive observance of life and found what little relief I could by communicating to myself through prose and poetry. I was trying desperately to find where I fit in life, but I was slowly coming to the conclusion that I didn't fit anywhere.

Lacking direction and feeling like my life was going nowhere, I decided to stop avoiding the draft and tried to enlist in the military. I wanted to get it over with and do my duty. However, my juvenile arrest record caused the Air Force and then the Navy to reject my applications. With great uncertainty and hesitation, I volunteered to be drafted into the U.S. Army. Although the men at the enlistment office promised and signed an agreement stating I would not be inducted until the end of the summer, two weeks later while visiting friends in the Midwest, I received my induction notice and was told to report immediately for my physical. This was the first indication that perhaps the military was as untrustworthy as every other established system of authority I had known!

By the time I had hitch-hiked back to the West Coast, I was certain I did not want anything to do with the military and devised a well-rehearsed scheme to fail the physical. Unfortunately, I passed anyway. Since the conflict in Vietnam was escalating, they were taking anything that walked on two legs and barked.

My experience in Basic Training and Advanced Military Training only confirmed my suspicions about the military. Harassed, intimidated, humiliated, threatened, abused and betrayed, I doggedly resisted every attempt by those in authority to break my spirit. I was determined not to yield to what I saw as corrupt, insensitive and bullying leadership, and I often paid the price for it. I learned both the cost and rewards of standing alone.

However, I also learned to carry deep respect and quiet loyalty for those who proved themselves to be capable, caring, and courageous leaders. Furthermore, I became increasingly aware of my own abilities and found new strength when others saw me as competent and resourceful. I earned both the loyalty and respect of others. Even though I did my best to avoid it, I found myself repeatedly being thrust into positions of leadership and responsibility. Then came Vietnam!

Journey into hell.

Vietnam was, for me, a head-long plummet into hell! A series of highly personalized experiences marked the way. What had been a naive, care-free, irresponsible existence suddenly became a life-and-death struggle—characterized by "survival at any cost." I had not known whether the war was right or wrong, but I had trusted my country. Thrust into combat, what I thought was "noble and good" became disastrous and ugly. Mere words can never explain either the depth of terror or the exalted triumph of human will after surmounting overwhelming odds in the face of death. In the killing fields of Vietnam, hyper-vigilance superseded rest. Guilt replaced innocence.

As the death toll mounted, so did my mistrust of my government and military leadership. I felt betrayed. My descent into the pit of sin and human depravity was equal only to the heightened sense of loyalty, commitment, and iron-clad devotion soldiers develop toward one another.

Claustrophobic, chaotic, violent—the war turned to long months of near-suffocating heat and painful exhaustion. Fear turned to hardened rage and cold-hearted, calculated struggle just to survive. There were times when I wanted to break down and weep from exhaustion and discouragement. But despite disillusionment, I hung on, believing it would soon be over and I could return to a world where I could put the terror, suffering, and inner turmoil behind me. I would never have to think of it again. That one focus kept me from losing heart, losing hope, and giving in to despair. Unfortunately, it did not keep me from having a break-down in the field, nor did it keep me from turning to drugs in desperate attempts to keep my sanity.

Coming home.

When the day finally came for departure from Vietnam, the long plane ride home was filled with a heavy sense of foreboding. I was not the same person who had left thirteen months earlier. The U.S. was fraught with growing conflict and strife over the war. I wondered how I would be accepted back home. Nevertheless, there was underlying hope and expectation that the war was now over for me. I would never have to think of it again. How foolish I was!

My homecoming was met with protest, cat-calls and sneers. I had to sneak back into my own country under cover of darkness for fear I would be attacked, spit on, or have blood thrown on me by those who were protesting the war at the front gates of military installations.

Within six months of my discharge, I collected a string of in-
dignities I found most difficult to bear. I was called a liar for saying
I had served in the military in Vietnam. I was "carded" at every bar,
refused service because people would not believe I was twenty-one,
even though I had an ID to prove it. I was jumped by a gang of six
teenagers who waved a hunting knife in my face and wanted to cut
my hair. They laughed when I told them I was a loyal patriot who
had just served his country in Vietnam. I was beaten up, spit upon,
and called a filthy communist.

As a result, I was bitterly angry and deeply resentful of my
country's betrayal, its ungratefulness, and its despicable treatment
and rejection of its young men who had given their best to serve
their country. Finally, I said to myself, *"America, you can go to
hell! You don't want me and I don't need you!"* In bitter rejection,
I turned my back on my country.

Now I had come full circle. I was totally isolated and alienated
from everyone except a few close friends and other Vietnam veterans. My mistrust and guardedness had become all-inclusive. I had
generalized my personal hurt until I was condemning an entire nation.

I became a recluse. I burned my uniform and hid every vestige
of my military experience. I roamed the country looking for a place
to belong and for people who could be trusted. I hid my past and
carried my guilt, never discussing my life as a soldier with anyone.

Six months later I was living in the Midwest, deeply embroiled
in the Vietnam protest movement. I saw my country, its government, and every established institution it represented as my enemy,
and I wished for its ultimate overthrow and destruction. I fought
the system with a vengeance and rebelled against every kind of
authority. I threw myself into an alternative life-style, believing with
youthful naiveté that we could develop an alternative society.

A year and a half after my discharge, I could no longer ignore
my recurring nightmares. I lived with a rifle at my bedside and had
serious difficulty sleeping. I jumped at every unexpected noise and
wept openly whenever television news covered the war in Vietnam.
Unable to form any kind of lasting relationships, I recoiled from
intimacy like a wounded animal. To numb my emotions, I became

entrenched in the use of marijuana. I would rather be "stoned" than eat.

When I visited a Veterans' Medical Center in search of treatment, the psychiatrist told me Vietnam had nothing to do with what I was feeling! He labeled me as paranoid with a developmental personality disorder. He thought I was just trying to get free medication and said I should try Zen meditation.

That was the final blow. If a professional doctor didn't think Vietnam had anything to do with why I felt so screwed up, then I would take it upon myself to put everything I had ever known or experienced behind me. I walked away from life in the city, my friends and acquaintances, and tried to start anew. I suppressed the pain and anger and screwed the lid on tight. I told myself that Vietnam was behind me now and I could get on with my life.

First steps toward real healing.

As the years passed, things did get better. I discovered a personal relationship with Jesus Christ, got married, and had a son. I became involved in a street ministry and later, in Christian community. Believers with maturity and depth of insight provided godly counsel and ministry to my wife and me. I began to experience healing from some of the broken relationships in my past. God began a process of healing, restoration, and reconciliation between me and my parents.

However, there were still problems in my relationship with my wife. She was hurt by my painful inability to open myself to her with complete vulnerability and trust. She always felt closed out of areas of my life I allowed no one to penetrate. I always had to have my emotions under control. It was difficult for me to bond with others, including my son. I went from job to job, none lasting more than three to six months. I was either fired or quit, mostly due to conflict with authority.

I still carried deep distrust of the government and was critical, condemning, and quick to uncover its weaknesses. I was also guarded and mistrusting toward nearly everyone else. Whenever I saw other veterans marching in patriotic parades, anger and revulsion filled the pit of my stomach. I constantly battled general unrest and fantasized continually about dropping out in hermetic isolation.

In 1979 I realized that my Vietnam experiences were not resolved. The war still had its inner aftermath. I began having excru-
ciatingly painful flashbacks, memories, and nightmares. I often wept
for seemingly no reason. I began having problems sleeping again
and thought I was falling apart physically. I went into the VA hospi-
tal for an Agent Orange examination and they told me they thought
I was having problems with post-traumatic stress disorder. I didn't
even know what that was. All I knew was that I couldn't stop the
memories from coming back no matter what I did, and I couldn't
hold back the tears.

Weathering a crisis of faith.

During this time my faith in God was severely tested and I went
through a spiritual crisis. This was a wrenching time, but it resulted
in my discovering the depth of God's forbearance and love. I finally
came to the conclusion that God had established our relationship on
a firm enough foundation so I could weather the painful process of
reconstructing my experience in Vietnam in order to achieve His
healing.

Encouraged by a Christian counselor/mentor, I began the painful process of writing a journal to record the memories that began
to flood my waking hours. I also began to meet again with other
Vietnam veterans. For the next ten years I wrote my memoirs of
Vietnam. That cleansing exercise included some incredibly painful
periods, for as the memories surfaced I often became physically,
mentally, and emotionally incapacitated.

Bitter roots discovered.

In the middle of this process God brought my wife and me into
contact with John and Paula Sandford's ministry and teaching on
bitter root judgments. Our home-group decided to investigate these
teachings with the expressed purpose of applying whatever God
revealed to us through ministry to one another. With renewed understanding of how we can defile ourselves and others by the judgments we sow, we both began to apply the blood of Christ and His
death on the cross to our lives. God began doing deeper work,
healing us and setting us free from our past. I also could see the
application of these principles to my experiences in Vietnam. I be-

came determined to lock the door to my past with the key of forgiveness.

The process for me was simple, yet fearful and oftentimes extremely painful. The result proved to be very liberating. Whenever the Lord surfaced buried memories from Vietnam, I wrote them down. I allowed myself to feel either the pain or the anger I had previously suppressed. I allowed myself to grieve the loss of friends and play out the rage that still burned within my soul. With careful determination, I explored those situations and the people involved. I identified the people I had blamed and made a conscious choice to forgive each one. Sometimes individuals couldn't be singled out so I forgave them as groups. There were individual leaders, other soldiers I had personally struggled with, specific children, Vietnam and Viet Cong soldiers. Then there were groups like the government, the legislature, rich people in general, military leaders, the Army of the Republic of Vietnam, and the Viet Cong.

I asked Jesus, my Healer,
to release the Comforter to take my pain.
It was too heavy and crippling to continue to carry,
and I could not heal myself.

I needed to be comforted. For years I had been satisfied to wallow in self-pity and blame others for causing my pain. Self-pity had been the way I comforted myself because I would not allow myself to be comforted by others.

I understood the need to communicate what I was experiencing, but I didn't have a trusted group of fellow veterans to share my thoughts or feelings. I would often ask my home-group to pray for me but I wouldn't divulge any specifics. I didn't trust that "civilians" would be either sincerely interested or able to understand what I was going through without judging me. So what I did was write it all down. It was private, yet I held nothing back. I endeavored to be totally transparent.

Accepting accountability.

God was also gracious to me in that He gave me a dream, the interpretation of which led me to realize my accountability for ending up in Vietnam. This realization did much to tear down the strongholds of self-pity, blame, and victimization that characterized my attitude.

Eventually, I became free of the anger, resentment, and bitterness surrounding Vietnam. The "stress response" that had become ingrained in Vietnam began to dissipate as I learned to develop new perspectives. The emotional wounds that occurred in Vietnam began healing. I could look back without the pain. My identity, which had been tied to Vietnam, began to shift to that of a son of God.

Nevertheless, my guardedness toward people other than Vietnam veterans lingered on. I was still very self-protective and slow to disclose anything personal with others. I was not readily transparent and rarely vulnerable to anyone other than those who had proven to be trustworthy. When Americans began to give some measure of respect to those who served their country in Vietnam, I would not receive it. To me, I didn't need it. I had already learned to make my adjustment. It came too little, too late! I wouldn't march in any parades. I wouldn't salute the flag. I wouldn't say the pledge of allegiance. On patriotic occasions, if anyone said, *"Thank you,"* I held their statement in the highest degree of skepticism.

Breaking free of my bondage to fear.
Then in 1992, during a Christian growth seminar called FOCUS, God exposed my guardedness in a way that revealed itself actually to be bondage to fear. I knew it was rooted in the mistrust and unforgiveness I still held toward *all* Americans for the way I was treated when I returned from Vietnam. I knew what God was requiring of me—I had a choice to make, and choose I did.

I asked the seminar group to represent for me all the Americans I still hated because of the rejection I had experienced. I asked them to forgive me. Then, I gave them my forgiveness. I allowed them to comfort me with their love and repentance. God brought deep healing and reconciliation on the spot, not just for me but for everyone involved in the group.

I still stand amazed at the new freedom and liberty that choice brought into my life. The presence of God and the anointing of the Holy Spirit brought such a time of refreshment, I continue to walk in it today. Since I was finally reconciled to America, the Spirit of

God could flow through me with new vigor. I could touch the lives of others in a way I had never been able to. The Spirit of God had been hindered by my unwillingness to walk before others in humility, openness, transparency, and vulnerability.

It was not that I had to trust other people more than I had, it was that I learned to trust God in a new way in my life. I saw that my choice to be vulnerable was my own. Transparency was my own. No one could take it from me. It was mine to give and take back whenever I wanted. What freedom and release there was in forgiveness!

I have come to see how developing patterns of experiences and choices can lead us to avoid, deny, or suppress our anguish. Thus we are progressively drawn into suffocating bondage. Bondage originates with offenses (injuries, wounds, bruisings). Jesus said to His disciples:

Things that cause people to sin are bound to come. . .
(Luke 17:1)

Life without suffering is impossible and anyone who lives running from pain lives no life at all. When we are injured by others, or by injustice, the natural response is anger. It is not merely natural, it is quite normal. We are hurt when we are treated unjustly. When others disrespect us, or treat us with insensitivity, they violate God's intent. The fact that we get angry is, if anything, a response which reflects the nature and character of our God who gets angry at sin. But when we don't show love or regard for one another, that also is sin.

In your anger do not sin. Do not let the sun go down while you
are still angry, and do not give the devil a foothold.
(Ephesians 4:26)

Our problem is not anger. Our problem is that we don't resolve our anger every day, and therefore end up sinning. Unresolved angers, carried day after day, become resentment. Resentments, once ingrained in the heart, become bitterness. Jesus called bitterness a "hardened heart." It is the root cause of much trouble.

See to it that no one misses the grace of God and that no bitter root grows up to cause trouble and defile many.

(Hebrews 12:15)

Making the choice to forgive.

In anger we have a choice. We can communicate with those who offended us and forgive them, or we can hold on to their sin and walk in unforgiveness, resentment, and bitterness. Jesus said:

So watch yourselves. If your brother sins, rebuke him, and if he repents, forgive him. If he sins against you seven times in a day, and seven times comes back to you and says, I repent, forgive him. *(Luke 17:3-4)*

We can choose to keep our hearts open, making ourselves available to be touched by others, and giving of ourselves to them as well. Or, we can choose to harden our hearts, building walls around our heart so that we are no longer vulnerable.

Some of the characteristics of a hardened heart and a protective life-style are:

- guardedness
- self-centeredness
- emotional and social isolation and withdrawal
- insensitivity to others and to the Holy Spirit
- lack of understanding and insight
- a slumbering spirit or unawakened conscience
- critical, condemning perspectives on others and life
- loneliness
- alienation
- anger and rage
- a host of other destructive behaviors.

A life of unforgiveness is a life of bitterness and torment. It is a life which opens to demonic oppression. It is a life of bondage to addictions and compulsive behaviors which seek to gratify the flesh in some hope of alleviating constant emotional stress. It is a life of unrest and violence.

I can see clearly that God allowed me to go down the path of my own choosing and allowed me to suffer the consequences of my choices in order to turn me away from that path. Before Vietnam I was a free-thinker, a non-believer who was primarily a rationalist. In Vietnam my eyes were opened to the depravity of man and the results that are produced by a philosophy of the "survival of the fittest." I saw the nature of my own sin and depravity. It broke my heart and opened my mind. It forced me to look outside myself. It caused me to pursue a knowledge of God.

From darkness to light.

How does my life parallel others? Maybe yours is also a life of bitterness and resentment toward the rich. Maybe you are trapped in a life of poverty and the very people you resent (those you have closed off all relationship with) are the same ones God has ordained to bring you out of poverty.

Maybe yours is a life of bitterness and suspicion toward black people, or white. Maybe you distrust or dislike the people in your church, or all Christians in general. Maybe you are disgusted with "liberals" or can't stomach "conservatives." Perhaps your broken marriage or other hurts in your life have left you distrustful and hostile toward all men, or all women. It doesn't matter what group upon whom you have generalized your anger and resentment. By your anger, you have alienated yourself.

> *Anyone who claims to be in the light but hates his brother is still in the darkness. . . he does not know where he is going because the darkness has blinded him.* (1 John 2:10-11)

A life-style of unforgiveness pollutes our life and defiles others. It results in spiritual, mental and emotional darkness. The good news is that God forgives us, and He wants us to forgive others. We can walk in the light because Jesus is light and He came to show us the way. If we love one another, we abide in the light and the light is what keeps us from stumbling.

Grace, mercy, and forgiveness express God's nature and character to others. If we do not "fall short of the grace of God," His light directs us on our path to a full and meaningful life. Forgiveness is the key that sustains the light and enables us to walk down the path to total healing.

Giving and receiving forgiveness.

Healing starts by identifying those who have offended us and choosing to grant them forgiveness. Give, and you shall receive full measure, pressed down, and shaken together. In the same measure we give to others, God gives to us.

Healing continues as we seek to be forgiven. We must ask God to forgive us for living in resentment and allowing our hearts to become hardened. We must ask for forgiveness from those whom we have defiled by our own bitterness.

Then, we must allow ourselves to be comforted.

Praise be to the God and Father of our Lord Jesus Christ, the Father of compassion and the God of all comfort, who comforts us in all our troubles, so that we can comfort those in any trouble with the comfort we ourselves have received from God.   *(2 Corinthians 1:3-4)*

The Holy Spirit of God is our comforter, but we must allow others to comfort us as well.

. . . speaking the truth in love, we will in all things grow up into Him who is the Head, that is, Christ. From Him the whole body, joined and held together by every supporting ligament, grows and builds itself up in love, as each part does its work.   *(Ephesians 4:15-16)*

Confession, exposure, openness, and transparency with others you trust can bring about greater healing than you can ever achieve alone.

Is any one of you in trouble? He should pray. Is anyone happy? Let him sing songs of praise. Is any one of you sick?

He should call the elders of the church to pray over him and anoint him with oil in the name of the Lord. And the prayer offered in faith will make the sick person well; the Lord will raise him up. If he has sinned, he will be forgiven. Therefore, confess your sins to each other and pray for each other so that you may be healed. The prayer of a righteous man is powerful and effective. (James 4:13-16)

Start by conducting a personal inventory of your unforgivenesses. If you cannot identify the specific offenses behind your general attitude toward yourself or others, then ask the Holy Spirit to search your heart and mind. He will bring those things hidden in the dark recesses of your past to the light. Seek the help of trusted Christian counselors, those trained in their senses to discern right from wrong and good from evil.

Draw unto Christ and He will draw unto you. God is faithful!

What then are the lessons each of us can learn from the unforgivenesses we have allowed to linger in our life? When our responses to life's challenges leave us wallowing in a pigpen of unhappiness, what are we to do? We have the option of holding on to the hurt, rehearsing our anger, and nurturing our bitterness. That is the lesson so much of the world teaches—seek justice through revenge and look for satisfaction in vindictiveness. But that choice is empty, perverse and destructive. Nations rage against nations, and wounded people trade grudge for grudge. All is vanity.

There is real hope only for those who are willing to cry out: *"Oh Lord, have mercy upon me, for I am a sinner! Have mercy upon us, for we are all sinners!"*

In repentance, humility and trust in God's healing love, we must be willing to *choose forgiveness* and seek the Lord's help as we take our own long journey home.

Merciful Father God,

I cry out to You from my weakness and sin, recognizing that without the awful sacrifice made for us by the Lord Jesus Christ on the cross, I could never hope to come before Your throne of mercy and grace.

Like the prodigal son, I have squandered so much of Your treasure. I have rebelliously followed so many paths that have led only to darkness and destruction. Forgive me for those foolish ways.

My eyes now seek a continuing vision of Your warm light penetrating those places where cold fog of confusion may obscure the proper pathway on my journey home.

If I should falter and become distracted by the pain of hurtful relationships, please grant me strength and courage through Your Holy Spirit to endure along the way—always to choose the higher ground of forgiveness and reconciliation.

Loving Father, be my comforter, guardian, guide, and stay. I ask in Jesus' name.

Amen

Life Application:
The Pigpen Dilemma
Making Personal Peace in an Unjust World

This chapter gives us a glimpse into the lives of two people, revealing how their hearts grew bitter with hate and unforgiveness and what they did to overcome those problem issues. Review these stories to evaluate for yourself the significance of their struggles and their triumphs. Discuss these issues with your group.

Concerning Charlie Finck's story—
♦ What was the basic reason for Charlie's insecurity and bitterness? (See pages 27-28)

♦ How did the bitterness of his youth effect him when he left home to go to college? (See pages 28-29)

♦ What is the significance of the prayer Charlie learned to pray? What elements of this prayer began to make a difference in changing his feelings toward his father? (See page 30)

♦ When Charlie made the decision to sow an attitude of forgiveness, what results did he begin to reap in his life? (See page 31)

Concerning Howard Olsen's story –
Howard traces a journey of many years during which he persevered to find ways to overcome the bitterness that had burdened his life.

♦ What effect did it have for Howard to identify each situation that had brought him pain and make a decision to forgive? (See pages 39-40)

♦ What did Howard ask the Holy Spirit to do in his life and why did this seem necessary? (See page 40)

♦ What effect did accepting accountability for his attotudes and actions have on how Howard began to feel? (See page 40)

♦ What role did repentance play in coming into an attitude of forgiveness? (See page 41)

Continue your personal journey toward forgiveness.
Conduct a personal inventory of your unforgivenesses. Be specific about people and events you need to choose to forgive.

Forgiveness needs:

Chapter Three

Facing Truth and Reality
Where We Are on the Journey Toward Forgiveness

Holding on to holiness	HOLDING ON TO WHOLENESS
Gripping tight the day	GIVING THANKS FOR FREEDOM
The rules came down	TO FORGIVE AND BE FORGIVEN
Spelling out the texts	AND ALLOWING LOVE
That make one pure	TO BRIDGE THE BROKENNESS
Laying down the mind	FILLING EMPTY HOURS
Waiting for the end of time	WITH REVERENCE
Holding on to holiness	LIVING THE TIME OF OUR LIVES
With white knuckles	HOLDING ON TO WHOLENESS
And a quivering chin	WITH OPEN ARMS
Scared to death	AND OPEN MINDS
Unto death	FREE TO LIVE
Into death	ABLE TO GIVE
That we'll be caught	WALKING WITH CONFIDENCE
With our bags unpacked	THAT TOMORROW'S NEEDS
When God's big ship	WILL BE MET TOMORROW
Comes in	FOR THOSE WHO LIVE
Holding on to holiness	FAITHFULLY WITH JOY TODAY
Until it becomes a sin	HOLDING ON TO WHOLENESS
	AND LETTING GRACE COME IN

Lee Bowman

J esus told a story about a wealthy man who forgave his servant a debt of ten thousand talents. Soon after being forgiven his debt, the servant came across a man who owed him just one talent. He confronted the man and said, *"Pay me!"* When the man said he could not pay, the servant took him by the throat and threatened him. The master heard of the incident and called his servant, saying, *"I forgave you ten thousand talents and you would not forgive this man even one!"* The master then ordered the servant to be severely punished and all his debts to be placed back on him. (Matthew 18:21-35)

Of course the moral of Jesus' story is that we must respond to the wonderful grace of God's forgiveness by extending that same grace of forgiveness to others. If we do not, our sins will surely rebound on us in crushing ways.

Forgiveness not really given.

The difficult thing about forgiveness is that we often think we have forgiven when in reality we have not. Most people are neither aware, nor will they readily admit, that they haven't forgiven others. We give lip service to having forgiven, but then we harbor grudges in our heart. Most of us labor under the difficulty of really letting go of our hurts. In fact we sometimes seem quite proud of our grudges.

People often say something like: *"I'm willing to be Christian about it and turn my cheek once, or maybe even twice, but after that, they had better watch out!"*

Or, perhaps to justify anger and unforgiveness: *"I'd be willing to forgive him for an honest mistake, but he meant to hurt me."*

The central daily work of a Christian

Anger and unforgiveness destroy life. As Christians, forgiveness must be our central daily work if we are to guard our hearts against hate and bitterness and walk in love with Jesus.

Every speck of dust we see
in the eye of a brother or sister must be measured
against the great splatters of mud
that cloud our own vision.

Most of the time we take forgiveness for granted. We make an effort to forgive and think we are free of the hurt, but then a situation comes up that triggers old emotions, and we are back into the hurt and bitterness again. We fool ourselves when we think enlightened will power is enough to overcome dark resentments, jealousies, bitternesses, and fears we have held inside for so long. As Christians, we should recognize that unforgiveness is a sin issue which cannot be remedied through our striving. We can spend all of our emotional energy trying to cope with our hurts and wind up frustrated over how little headway we have made in changing those deep feelings. Without the power of the Lord Jesus Christ, we can expect little relief.

Forgiveness only gets done
when it is taken to the cross.

We naturally expect anger and unforgiveness to be directed toward strangers who may have hurt us or toward those with whom we have not developed close relationships. The truth is that we are more likely to retain hurts from those who are close to us, such as a spouse, parent, child, or other family member. Whenever we experience hurt from those we care about the most, it is more difficult to be forgiving.

Marriage is the most vulnerable relationship in which hurt and unforgiveness can happen. Happiness and success in marriage require exercise in the art of forgiveness twenty-four hours a day, 365 days a year.

Let us share with you some of the things we have learned about forgiveness, both through our own marriage, and through many years of counseling others.

Four levels of wounding that require forgiveness.

1. Bruise: *Surface level wounding which can be healed easily if treated promptly and properly. Bruises or abrasions require forgiving moment by moment.*

It is relatively easy to forgive people when we understand that the hurts were not malicious acts. We realize people were just insensitive, made errors in judgment, unthinkingly had a slip of the tongue or inadvertently slighted us. Even though the events caused some pain, we know they weren't something done premeditatively or out of spite. Feelings can be caught before they get out of hand, and an irritable response in retaliation can be avoided. It's like saying, *"This act wasn't intentional. Taking an angry and unforgiving stance is unjustified. I will clearly make my feelings known and choose to be forgiving."*

If we don't take ourselves too seriously, many of those unintentional hurts can be dealt with by applying humor. We need to sort through our feelings and learn the difference between situations that require a real miracle of forgiveness and those that can be caught on the fly and dispatched with a sprinkling of light-hearted grace. By catching feelings as we experience them, we can keep problems in perspective and avoid hooking into whatever other feelings are left in our heart that haven't yet been dealt with by the Lord.

🍎 *Paula: Unthinking acts*

An illustration of this is the irritation we used to have in our family over letting pets in the house. John used to feel sorry for our dog Holly who would beg at the door. John would let Holly in and then forget she was inside. Later when we had gone to bed and were all snuggled down for the night, we would begin hearing weird sounds—of a dog eating house plants and chewing on furniture! Holly was teething. Left alone in the house, she chewed on whatever was available.

This was very irritating to me. Each time it happened, I had to exercise a choice whether or not to forgive John's lack of awareness and his lack of responsibility. I would tell myself that John let the dog in, but he did not intend for the dog to do all those destructive things.

Since this happened again and again, forgiveness became a struggle, but it got easier as I reminded myself that the issue of John letting the dog stay in the house at night was not all there was to our marriage. The destructive thing that often happens in marriages is that each partner allows the irritation of the moment to become so intense as to respond in ever-increasing levels of anger and resentment until both become tyrannized by the feelings of the moment.

John . . . Catching irritants in life and dispatching them moment by moment does not mean that we just dismiss irritants as unimportant. They may not be worth elevating to a major issue, but they must be dealt with on some level rather than just stuffing them down inside. This usually means simply making the other persons aware of issues, hurts, or disappointments, and telling them that we are willing to forgive if they are willing to ask forgiveness. And then learning to forgive instantly anyway, even if they are unwilling to ask for forgiveness or even admit they were at fault.

When someone asks to be forgiven, don't say, *"It's okay"* It's not okay. The offender needs to hear the words, *"I forgive you."* If we excuse hurts by saying it's okay, we may be indicating that what the person did had no power to affect us—that the person is not important to us.

Forgiveness is a necessary, moment-by-moment, day-by-day exercise because letting little things mount up creates the proverbial mountain out of a mole hill. Paula had to learn not to say, *"It's okay,"* but instead, *"It's not okay what you did, John, but I forgive you. And honey, would you please pay better attention next time?"*

🍓 *Paula: Insensitivity*

We put in a vegetable garden almost every year, which has consistently been the talk of the neighborhood because God has blessed it so beautifully. John has always been proud of our garden. In the early years of our marriage he was so anxious and excited to share our bounty that he would daily gather the ripened produce and bring it all into the kitchen. Piling it all over the table and cabinets, he would say with great enthusiasm, *"Look, honey, aren't we blessed!"*

Surveying that mountain covering every available space in the kitchen, I would feel anything but blessed—and my response reflected it. When the corners of my mouth went down and the pitch of my voice went up, John felt like I was raining on his parade. He felt I didn't appreciate his gifts—or him.

I chose to forgive him in the moment for not realizing how overwhelming it was to me. Subsequently, John learned not to bring all the produce into the kitchen, but to put it on a table on the back porch where I could take a little at a time and process what I could handle without feeling burdened. Then we could both share the joy of the bounty.

🍓 *Paula: Error in Judgment*

John has always had a propensity to lose track of time. When he was in the pastorate, he would be out calling on parishioners, and his stomach really had to rumble loudly before he remembered it was mealtime. He wore a wristwatch but he continually forgot to look at it. I would be at home, warming and re-warming the meal, steaming within myself.

Then he would crash through the door saying *"I'm starved to death!"* as though I had not already prepared the meal. Again and again, I chose to forgive on the fly so that things didn't get blown out of proportion.

When we forgive people, we expect it to have the desired effect. They should learn the lesson. The next time the offensive act happens, it's harder to forgive because apparently they didn't learn the lesson. What we need to understand about forgiveness is that it seldom results in the offending party doing an about face.

For twelve years, I served overcooked scorched meals, and had to keep on choosing forgiveness. If forgiveness isn't at the center of a marriage, you just can't make it.

Surprisingly, when I learned to forgive and not make such a big issue out of his tardiness, he was more able to remember meal times. Then when he did become tardy, he would pop in the door and say something like, *"Oh honey, I'm sorry. I lost track of time. Will you forgive me?"*

🍎 *Paula: Unintentional Hurt*

John loves to bring people home for dinner—unannounced! Usually that's okay, because with six kids around we almost always had plenty of food prepared. On one particular occasion John brought a friend, Mike. For Mike, coming to dinner at our house was a special treat. He came all dressed up, bearing a gift. John had forgotten to tell me Mike was coming! On that particular day all we had was left-over hamburger casserole! I was embarrassed and had to try hard to be forgiving. Though John neglected to tell me, it was not intentional.

John is still too quick to invite someone to dinner or to spend the week-end. Sometimes he doesn't stop to count the empty beds or to check our schedule. For a long time, when John would do this, I would laugh a "gallows laugh," suppressing my anger, and make do. Then I began to forgive and actually chuckle when it would happen.

Forgiveness for life's constant unintentional hurts is not only a necessary discipline, it is what keeps the joy of love in relationships.

---

2. Cut: *More serious wound that perhaps was inflicted intentionally. The hurt produces immediate, personal pain and will require special treatment to achieve forgiveness and healing.*

Think about it. What situation is most likely to cause your emotional temperature to rise—your three-year-old accidentally bumping over a glass of milk at the dinner table, or your three-year-old looking you straight in the eye and deliberately pushing over a glass of milk? Normally, we're able to deal calmly with a child's "devilish" behavior, but when an adult peer does something we interpret as deliberately hurtful, we really have to work at being willing to forgive. Hurts which cause crises of forgiving usually have three characteristics:

- The hurt is personal
- The wounding act seems very unfair
- The pain is felt deeply

Each of the three tends to complicate our ability to move toward forgiveness. When someone else is hurt, we can be more understanding or objective toward the dynamics of the situation because we don't feel the pain personally. But when we're the object of the wounding, there is no emotional buffer. The affront is firsthand, the injustice is ours to bear, and subsequent feelings penetrate. The more personal the hurt and the more unjust the act, the more difficult the task of calling forth the will to forgive.

This kind of wounding often occurs when we have been passed over for a job promotion we feel we deserved, when we are slighted by a friend and not included in a group or activity, when a parent or other family member shows favoritism, or when we generally feel discounted or undervalued by someone we care about. We feel the "cut" when we suffer the consequences of someone else's selfishness, when they deliberately do something to "get even" with us, or when we feel they have deliberately tried to embarrass us by making us look bad.

Forgiveness must always begin with a choice—a willingness to realistically assess both our own and the other person's accountability, and then release resentment about the one who wronged us so that we ourselves might be healed of the hurts. Once we understand the destructive nature of unforgiveness and the lingering poison it infuses into our spirits, we should desire to choose forgiveness out of the pure logic of its benefits.

3. Open Wound: *Major hurt lodged in the heart that cannot be treated just by our own understanding or desire to change our feelings. The pain continues despite our consciously wanting to forgive.*

When we have been intentionally hurt by a person unrepentant of the injury, we are less motivated to forgive at the time of the wounding. The hurt becomes a constant affront to us. The wound festers, we become resentful, and deep resentment or bitterness sets in. When feelings overcome reason and resentments penetrate so deeply that choosing to forgive seems impossible, then our unforgiveness has become "lodged in the heart."

Our sister, Sue, experienced the intensity of this kind of personal pain when during an argument precipitated by divorce proceedings, her estranged husband pulled a favorite family photo from her refrigerator door and ripped it to pieces in her presence. That callous act penetrated deeply into her heart, not because of the value of the photo, but because of who did it and the way the act was maliciously intended to cause pain by showing disdain for her family.

Similar scenarios are acted out in the lives of thousands of people daily. A cutting remark designed to embarrass one's spouse in front of friends. A trusted friend violating a confidence for his or her personal gain. A jilted lover telling lies to soil the reputation of a former sweetheart. A fellow employee sabotaging the work of a colleague in order to make themselves look good and get his or her job. A trusted employee embezzling money. One sibling purposely not inviting another to an important family gathering. One member of the family selfishly taking more than their share of an inheritance after the death of a parent. These are the kinds of personal affronts that can hurt deeply. Unless they are dealt with quickly and thoughtfully, the wounded feelings can fester into bitterness.

> **We may consciously want to forgive**
> **because we recognize the benefits of forgiveness,**
> **but our wanting is not enough.**

Overcoming unforgiveness at such a deep level is extremely difficult. A desire to be forgiving is still essential to begin the process, but the actual achievement of forgiveness is something we must learn to turn over to the Lord to accomplish for us. We are, in a sense, driven to the cross.

> *Can the Ethiopian change his skin or the leopard his spots?*
> *Neither can you do good who are accustomed to doing evil.*
> *(Jeremiah 13:23)*

We cannot dislodge growing roots of resentment and bitterness (our spots) by ourselves. We must learn how to let the Lord Jesus Christ rid us of hurts that have taken root at such a deep level.

We may not always be aware of how negative our feelings are because what the mind does to handle hurtful situations is often a puzzle, even to ourselves. When we are wronged by another person and do not handle the situation with forgiveness, we also may not respond in anger immediately. We might say, *"Oh, that's all right,"* or *"It doesn't really matter."* With good intentions, we suppress our anger and then later spend time rehearsing what we should have said to the offender. By that time, bitter feelings have sent down deep roots.

Christians are taught to be loving, thoughtful, and forbearing, so we often try to handle hurtful situations through rationality alone. We think forgiveness can be accomplished simply by mental choice, or that time and distance will heal all things. We sublimate feelings and rationalize hurtful situations by saying something like, *"He's always so busy he just forgets."*

Or, we try to understand why someone might choose to hurt us and we decide to be compassionate. *"He's really mean spirited, but I guess that's just the way he was raised."* We think our choosing to act compassionately accomplishes forgiveness. But in fact, forgiveness is not done until we take our hurts to the cross, giving our deep feelings to the Lord for Him to put to death and to restore a right spirit in us.

At the heart of the model prayer (Matthew 6:9-13) is the request for God to forgive us as we forgive our debtors (or our abusers). It takes a lot of humility to pray that part. *"Forgive me as much as I forgive my abusers? Are you kidding, Lord?"*

No, He's not kidding. But He will help us forgive, because forgiving abusers requires supernatural help.

When God asks us to forgive abusers, some will misunderstand Him to mean that the abuser will get off without penalty. This is not true because God provides judgment and renders justice far better than we can do. God loves us and does not want us to suffer. He wants us to be free of the pain of abuse and free of the pain we bring upon ourselves through our own vengeful judgment.

The Lord Jesus Christ took the vengeance of all mankind to the cross, but only those will be forgiven who submit their lives to Him who died for their sins. All others will have to reap the full measure of penalty for the grief they sow. We should leave vengeance to be handled by the Lord.

This process of giving our unforgiveness to the Lord has no simple formula from which we can always expect immediate and surprising results, but there is a discipline of faith which we must follow. We must trust in the Lord Jesus Christ as Savior. We must accept Him as the Son of God who has authority and power to forgive sins, to overcome death, and to make us into new beings. We must come to Him repentantly so that we become malleable spirits in whom Jesus can work His transforming miracle.

Coming into the reality of forgiveness may require returning in prayer to the Lord again and again, each time old feelings emerge. We can fool ourselves into believing forgiveness is accomplished and rationalize away our feelings. One of the best tests whether forgiveness is accomplished is when someone starts criticizing the person who caused our hurt and we have no desire to add to it.

---

4. Crippling Injury: *Deep wounds of the spirit resulting in pervasive attitudes of unforgiveness toward life. The actual wound or its ramifications may not be in one's conscious awareness.*

Traumatic experiences of early childhood can be imprinted in the spirit and cause difficulty in adolescent, teen, and adult years, even though there may be no conscious remembrances of the traumas. For example, when a child is given up for adoption, the child's personal spirit knows it and the spirit grieves for the natural parents. This grieving must be dealt with as a process of forgiveness, but it is difficult to accomplish in a young child who does not yet know how to distinguish those feelings and give them over to Jesus.

A child born into a family under financial stress or emotional turmoil among family members may be deprived of the love, attention and positive nurture required to build basic trust. This can result in deep-seated responses of feeling abandoned or angry toward parents. Such unforgivenesses lodged deep in the spirit are often expressed in destructive behaviors that do not seem to be immediately connected to the early childhood trauma. The root cause of those woundings needs to be uncovered and forgiveness accomplished in order to produce healing. This search from "fruit to root" will often require help from an experienced Christian counselor to reveal the source of hidden woundings and to initiate the healing process through forgiveness.

When emotional, physical, or sexual abuse has been experienced as a young child, and the child has suppressed such extremely hurtful feelings as a means of survival, the hurts remain deeply lodged in the heart and spirit. If we were abused growing up (and we all were to some extent) then we have shame. As children, we thought we must really be bad kids to deserve this kind of treatment. This shame is false guilt.

As adults, we continue to carry that shame and continue to stuff our feelings to avoid bringing the memories to consciousness. We may also develop addictive behaviors to keep our minds and feelings off the pain of that false guilt. We carry that pain until we see the truth and begin the process to forgive the abuser and ourselves.

Such emotional scars can cause continuing problems throughout life unless dealt with in a decisive way through the intercession of Jesus to accomplish forgiveness.

Not all childhood traumas are a result of intentional abuse. Oftentimes simple unthinking acts can be very devastating to a child. For example, a seven-year-old has been working all morning on a drawing, and she comes running to show it to her Daddy. She jumps into his lap and wants him to share in her pride and joy. But Daddy is in the middle of an exciting football game on TV. He pushes her aside angrily and scolds her for being in the way, making him miss an important play. His little girl's enthusiasm bursts like a balloon. She feels wronged and rejected.

How can a seven-year-old girl tell her Daddy how that makes her feel? She probably doesn't try. But that hurtful experience, and many more similar experiences, weigh heavily on her fragile spirit. She may eventually lose memories of individual events, but the cumulative effect becomes lodged in her being.

When hurts are so ingrained in the heart and spirit that they express themselves in bitter attitudes toward life, forgiveness is the toughest to accomplish, and release can seldom be achieved in one session of prayer. Forgiveness has to be worked at for a long time, with many prayers, in order to dislodge ingrained feelings and wash them away.

If your father ignored you when you were a young child, you probably developed a father vacuum. If your mother ignored you, you would tend to have a mother vacuum. These are like holes in our souls that cause us to crave love and attention. If parents don't fill the vacuum, other people can, and we must seek out the healthy nurturing places with those who can love us back to life.

We cannot depend on parents to nurture self-worth into us, and we should not cling to the fantasy that they will change someday and finally come through with the quality of love we need. Through Jesus we can cut the umbilical cord of dependence on unhealthy or incomplete nurture. We can submit to His love and be free because He shows us God, our heavenly Father, who alone is completely faithful and completely trustworthy to provide for our deepest needs.

More on the subject of how inadequate nurture can deaden one's spiritual sensitivity can be found in the book *Waking the Slumbering Spirit* by John and Paula Sandford and Norm Bowman (Clear Stream Publishing, 1993).

The chart on the next page gives an overview of four levels of wounds which result in unforgiveness, along with a description of the character of the pain commonly experienced and the response needed to work through the process of forgiveness.

Woundings and the forgiveness process

Wounds and Wounding Events	Characteristics of the Pain	Response Needed to Achieve Forgiveness
"Bruise" • Unintentional hurt • Insensitive act • Error in judgment • Slip of the tongue • Irritability, quarrelsomeness • Gossip * *Offender is immediately repentant when aware of offense.*	**Surface irritant** • Causes inconvenience • Creates distraction • Produces dissapointment • Temporarily affects openness • Short-term discomfort	**Forgive on the fly** • Consider the logical benefits of forgiving • Catch issues and deal with them in the moment • Relate to offender with light-hearted grace and sense of humor
"Cut" • Intentional wounding • Disloyalty • Unfairness • Dishonesty • Embarrassment • Getting even * *Offender becomes repentent when confronted*	**Hurt penetrates** • Feels like personal affront • Violates sense of justice • Feelings of being: Discounted Disrespected Unprotected Uncared for	**Proactively choose to forgive.** • Define boundaries and mutual accountabilities. • Choose forgiveness in the moment for repentant offenders. • Release hurts before they fester to bitterness • Seek reconciliation
"Open Wound" • Premeditated wounding • Malicious offense • Constant criticism • Selective withdrawal of affection • Bitter betrayal • Planned revenge • Public humiliation * *Offender is unrepentant and may continue behavior.*	**Pain becomes lodged in the heart** • Hurt is deeply personal • Pain rehearsed, obsessively • Wound festers • Blame is verbalized • Resentment becomes lodged in the heart	**Repent of judgments and take unforgiveness to the Lord as sin issues.** • Pray repeatedly for forgiveness to be accomplished • Depend on God • Estasblish clarity about future relationship • Bless those who hurt you • Patiently endure the long process of healing
"Crippling Injury" • Traumatic experiences in early childhood • Repeated over long period • Unresolved grief • Deprivation of love, nurture • Emotional, physical, or sexual abuse • Traumatic loss • Terror, being out of control * *Offender unrepentant and often not specifically identifiable*	**Deep wounds of the spirit** • Absence of basic trust • Feeling of abandonment • Deep-seated anger • Feeling of rejection • Mistrust and hostility • Powerlessness • Lingering anxiety • Pervasive fear • Victimization • Bitter attitude toward life • Isolation, withdrawal	**Seek help in tracing fruit to root.** • Acknowledge unforgiveness • Pray for inner healing, death to old self, and restoration • Replace old patterns with resurrected life • Bless those who hurt you. • Continue a commitment to choose forgiveness • Patiently endure the long process of healing

Is unforgiveness lodged in your heart?
Test yourself with these six questions.

1. Does remembering a particular hurtful event trigger a strong emotional reaction?

If thinking about a hurtful situation causes strong negative emotions or even physical shuddering, that suggests forgiveness is not complete. The hurt is still alive.

Many people fear reliving their hurts so they do their best to suppress all painful memories. They fool themselves into believing negative feelings will somehow go away: *"Maybe those old hurts will quit causing me pain if I just don't think about them."*

This often happens in cases of divorce, in fragmenting quarrels between siblings, or between parents and children. Rather than deal openly with conflict issues and work through forgiveness, people choose to cut themselves off from the conflict completely, as though the event never happened and as though the other person never existed.

We know of one Christian mother who was so upset that her daughter had chosen to marry a man of another race, she declared her daughter dead, insisted on holding a funeral, and forbade anyone in the family ever to speak of her again. Her racial prejudice, need to control others, and deep-seated unforgiveness continued for nearly twenty years, even after the death of her daughter's husband.

That kind of attitude is certainly no solution—especially in broken marriages where children are involved, or in families in which relationships cannot be separated without further hurting other family members who stand in the breach and love both alienated parties.

Time can be therapeutic, but it is not true that time heals all things. Painful experiences lodged in the heart have a way of springing to life again, triggering long-suppressed feelings.

See to it that no one comes short of the grace of God; that no root of bitterness springing up causes trouble, and by it many be defiled. *(Hebrews 12:15 NAS)*

You may think you have forgiven and forgotten. But if memories stir up another round of pain, it may be that you have merely worked hard at forgetting and forgiveness has not become complete. It is always better to accept the pain of remembering and endure the discipline of repeatedly choosing to forgive so the Lord can fully accomplish forgiveness in you. When forgiveness is complete, the memory of the event will no longer cause the pain. It can be seen as a valuable lesson learned and an illustration of the triumph of God's grace in producing healing and renewal.

2. Does the stress of remembering hurtful events trigger physical reactions or discomfort?
Memories of unforgiven events can often produce as much pain as the original event itself. Body language can be very telling. We should pay attention to how our body reacts physically when we think about a situation that caused pain in the past. Do shoulders tighten? Do teeth grind or fists clinch? Does the memory bring on indigestion or stomach cramps? Does the memory trigger depressive feelings or a desire to retreat into sleep? Is sleep disturbed? Or does the remembrance send us to the refrigerator for food to comfort our emptiness?

If remembering hurtful situations results in such physical symptoms, then unforgiven issues most likely remain lodged in the heart and spirit.

3. Does the painful experience bring to mind anything for which God can be praised?
Many of us have difficulty admitting we sometimes have anger toward God. We make mistakes, or we suffer because of the sins others inflict upon us, and then we hold God responsible.

A man's own folly ruins his life, yet his heart rages against the Lord.   *(Proverbs 19:3)*

We often deliver misdirected blame when we think what happened to us was unfair. We ask: "*Where was God if He's good and loving? Why did He let this awful thing happen? Why didn't He rescue me?"*

This is often the case when a child is stricken with a terminal illness, a family member is killed in a senseless automobile accident, or one's home burns to the ground. The unavoidable question is, *"Why did God let this happen?"*

We need to be honest by confessing to God our anger against Him. Of course God is not guilty of anything, and He is not in need of our forgiveness. Our anger and unforgiveness are our own. They grow out of the frustration we feel at being out of control. When unforgiveness is lodged in the heart, it is difficult to see any way God may be using the situation to bring blessing or to write wisdom into us. Afterwards, when we have achieved forgiveness, we can verbalize lessons learned and thank God for bringing us through painful experiences with a positive outcome.

For example, our aunt Irma Hedley who lived in Coffeyville, Kansas, tragically lost a young son when he went into shock during a routine tonsillectomy. At the time of her child's death, it was a grief almost too much to bear. But what grew out of that tragedy was Irma's development of a wonderful empathy for those suffering the loss of a loved one, and an ability to compassionately minister to them in their time of deepest need. For over fifty years she served as a veritable angel of mercy for those in her community who suffered tragic loss.

If forgiveness is complete, we will direct no blame toward God for what has happened to us. Our ability to enter into worship will be free and fulfilling. This can be a clue for us. When we praise God and anticipate a blessing from Him that does not come, one of the reasons may be that we are holding on to hidden anger toward Him. That blocks the blessing He has for us. If forgiveness is complete, our hearts will be open toward God and toward others.

When forgiveness is complete, we will enjoy the coming of a sense of relaxation about what happened to us. We learn from our experiences, not merely mentally, that God produces lessons of value in *any and all* circumstances of life.

*And we know that God causes all things to work together for
good to those who love God, to those who are called according to His purpose.*   *(Romans 8:28 NAS)*

**4. Can the offending party be thought of with a sincere
wish that good things will happen in his or her life?**
Forgiveness holds no grudges and wishes no penalties of retribution. It wipes clean the slate on which we formerly kept score
and allows us to wish only the best for the other person. Forgiveness restores love and promotes reconciliation. The apostle Paul
taught the bickering Corinthian church members:

*Love is patient, love is kind. It does not envy, it does not boast,
it is not proud. It is not rude, it is not self-seeking, it is not
easily angered, it keeps no record of wrongs.*
                                        (1 Corinthians 13:4-6)

We need to remember lessons learned through trials and hard-
ships for the sake of wisdom, but we should have no continuing
desire to keep score. Many people grant forgiveness in condescend-
ing ways while actually preserving mental catalogs of infractions. If
their provisional forgiveness is revoked later on, the list of past infractions is then produced as ready ammunition.

Forgiveness means letting go of grudges and bitternesses,
moving on without dragging baggage from the past. When forgiveness is complete, we can look back with relaxation and be able to
see something of value in the experience.

As well-known authors and leaders in a ministry, we have had
to endure difficult exercises in forgiveness because our ministry has
been attacked again and again, especially in an influential and
widely circulated book. The author, whom we have chosen not to
identify here, attacked our ministry and every other ministry having
anything to do with inner healing. Our first reaction was to become
furious because what he said about us in his book was not true. He
made many false assumptions which revealed he had not bothered
to research our books, or to find out what we were actually teaching.

Our greatest anger was because so many people who needed inner healing were being turned away by his false criticisms and the legitimate inner healing they had already experienced was being undermined. Disruption of meaningful ministry is still going on through the shadow of doubt cast by his attacks. The very concept of "inner healing" has become suspect in some circles.

Still today we find ourselves driven back to that daily discipline of forgiveness. We must continually choose to forgive and go to God in prayer to allow Him to accomplish in us what we cannot truly do on our own. The Lord says to us very clearly every day, *"FORGIVE! Unforgiveness is a poison. It doesn't produce life. It brings death. Bless the ones who persecute you."*

If we are dying due to our own unforgiveness, how are we going to bring life to anyone else?

> **If we want someone**
> **to change from darkness to light,**
> **we are to bless them and pray**
> **for goodness to come to them.**

When we forgive, we bless. We have chosen to do that. We pray blessing on the life of the one who has attacked us and we leave it up to God to decide what form that blessing will take.

> *Bless those who persecute you; bless and curse not.*
> *(Romans 12:14 NAS)*

For seven years Ami and Tony Lincoln lived next door to a neighbor in Coeur d'Alene who seemed impossible to get along with. Visitors coming to the Lincoln's home sometimes had to step off the narrow driveway onto his yard to get out of their cars and he made it known that he considered that an invasion of his property. The teenage boys at the Lincoln household were a special irritant to him in summer when they played their stereo music with the windows left open.

The sound of a hard-to-start motor on a winter morning was sure to inspire the neighbor's angry and profane words. One of the boys returning home late at night was once pursued from his car to the front door by this out-of-control "madman" wielding a baseball bat. He apparently was convinced the boy had committed some terrible deed. And from time to time, this neighbor was suspected of malicious property damage. The logic was: "Who else would have done a thing like that?" But in spite of the irritants, the Lincolns continued to choose forgiveness.

Then in the midst of this continuing neighborhood saga, the Lord spoke to Tony one day, saying: *"Bless him!"*

"But Lord!" Tony replied. *"You know we've forgiven him again and again."*

"I said bless him!" came the clear message again.

So Tony obediently began to bless his neighbor in prayer. During that same period of time the older of Ami and Tony's boys had a surprisingly peaceful talk with the neighbor which set the record straight on some past issues. And then the boy offered some used tire rims to the man. *"If they fit your car, you can have them."* They fit and he was thankful.

One day not long after that, the neighbor who was quite aware of the problem the Lincolns had growing grass under the big shade tree in their front yard, came over offering them half a bag of hybrid grass seed, especially formulated for shady lawns. *"It worked in my yard and I had this left over,"* he said.

Then the miracle began to grow. The man offered to show them how to get the grass to grow. He brought his tools to loosen the hard-packed soil. He scattered the seeds and raked them in. Then he roped off the area with stakes and twine and watered the freshly seeded lawn.

We had the privilege of watching this formerly hostile man as he obviously enjoyed the work he was doing for others. We marveled as he talked with the teenage boys as if they had long been buddies. What a wonder the Lord can work with our choices to bless and not curse!

5. Do you have a complete sense that forgiveness really has been accomplished?

Are you being honest with yourself about how you really feel? Is forgiveness coming from your heart, or do you find yourself saying something like, *"I did it Lord. You told me I had to do it. I made that choice, and I am a loving and forgiving person."* If you are forgiving primarily because you know you should, it may mean you are just going through the motions without forgiveness becoming a real part of you.

Check your feelings and symptoms. When you think about the persons who previously hurt you:

- Do you generally feel "okay" about them with no sense of lingering hurt or bitterness?
- Do you feel a loving warmth and desire for their success and happiness?
- Do you feel an empathetic hurt for their hurts without a private sense of pleasure that perhaps they are getting what they deserve?
- Do you miss having fellowship with them and wish you could restore relationship (even if wisdom says you can't)? If you happened to see them walking down the sidewalk toward you, would you be happy for the encounter, or would you want to cross the street to the other side, or duck into a store to avoid having to meet them?
- Are you able to feel comfortable about opportunities of being around them? If invited to a meeting or a party which they are likely to attend, would that spark a joy in your heart for the opportunity to see them, or would you decline to attend?

Before a comfort level can be reached toward those who have hurt us, it likely will require time, a conscious effort to redirect negative attitudes, and a lot of turning to the Lord for help in healing the wounded feelings. But ideally, forgiveness ultimately should produce reconciliation and perhaps even restoration of broken relationships.

❧ *Paula: Selfish and insensitive wounding*
We had a close friend in a parish years ago in whose home our children would go to play. She would bake them cookies and do other nice things for them. We opened our hearts to her. We were

vulnerable and risked with her. We shared with her and prayed with her about many things. Then we found out that she was circulating throughout the community, talking about the private things we had shared with her.

She also twisted some things that were said, and invented others which had never happened. She would state her own interpretations of events in our family life as though they were established facts. For example, when we were expecting our sixth child, she told people we did not want the baby. The truth was that this was a child we wanted and planned. But in her mind, she would not have wanted a sixth child so she told that story to others. This was a mild betrayal compared to many others, but it was especially painful because we had let her inside our family and our hearts. Somehow, her betrayal of confidentiality hurt more than any persecution we had experienced in the church.

For a long while, even though I wanted to forgive her and tried to identify with her feelings of insecurity that caused her to spread gossip, I had to choose again and again to ask the Lord to accomplish forgiveness in me. For a very long time I knew forgiveness wasn't accomplished because I could feel peaceful about her while away from her, but if I ran into her on the street or in a store, I would instantly feel uptight and would not go out of my way to greet her.

Overcoming this was a matter of going through a discipline of continued choices. I had to confess, *"Lord, I can't make this happen but you can make it happen in me."* Some time later after we had moved away from that town, we were back in the community and passed her house. We saw that the family was home and to my delight something of joy leaped up in me. We stopped and went in to see them. We had a very pleasant visit and I recognized at that time that the Lord had healed our hearts so that John and I could really open to her and embrace.

She never apologized for what she had done. She had needed to feel important and sharing these intimate things was a way she had of saying, *"Look, I'm on the inside with them."* It could be that she never realized how badly her actions had hurt us. That wasn't important, except perhaps for her and her relationship with the Lord. But the Lord managed to heal the hurt in us and there is no longer discomfort in our hearts when thinking about or being with her—though wisdom cautions us not to share those intimate things in our life which could tempt her to err again.

6. Is forgiveness producing positive results?

When a lifestyle of forgiveness is effectively achieved, it will produce wonderful fruits in the way we feel about ourselves and in the quality of relationships we are able to have with others. Conversely, lingering unforgivenesses result in insecurity, suspicion, criticism, and inability to be at peace with others and with ourselves. This is fact. It is one of the immutable laws of spiritual cause and effect so clearly unfolded for us in Scripture.

> *For if you forgive men when they sin against you, your heavenly Father will also forgive you. But if you do not forgive men their sins, your Father will not forgive your sins.*
> *(Matthew 6:14-15)*

> *A good tree cannot produce evil fruit, neither can an evil tree produce good fruit.* *(Matthew 7:17-18)*

The importance of self-forgiveness.

We characteristically have the most difficulty with others when our relationship with them triggers issues for which we have not forgiven ourselves. This is especially true between parents and children. For example, a father who regrets not having enough personal discipline to realize his own athletic potential as a teenager may be critical of his son's work ethic and experience resistance and difficulty with his son as he pushes him to excel in sports. Or, a mother who regrets wasting her own educational opportunities by partying in college may be judgmental of her fun-loving daughter and press her too heavily to be more disciplined and to excel academically.

Usually, weaknesses we see and criticize in others (and find most difficult to accept or forgive) are those things about which we have not forgiven ourselves, or in which we most fear being deficient. This is true in areas as divergent as personality traits, financial management, athletic prowess, or sexual behavior.

Look at what angers you in others. Look at the kind of person you just can't abide, and you will likely see something in yourself that you have been unable to forgive. As Christians we have many undiscovered pockets full of grudges and unforgivenesses. We have convinced ourselves we are clean when in actuality we may be seething inside with intolerance, fear and hate—much of which is focused on the reflection we see of ourselves as we encounter other people who in many ways are very much like us.

You therefore have no excuse, you who pass judgment on someone else, for at whatever point you judge the other, you are condemning yourself, because you who pass judgment do the same things.   *(Romans 2:1)*

Letting go of our denial and facing the truth about ourselves is a fearful step. The tension between the Holy Spirit pushing truth up and our fearful minds pushing the truth down is known as anxiety. It is the fear of the unknown. Part of us is wise and wants to know the truth. Part of us is foolish and fears the truth. The Holy Spirit will only bring healing to those who are willing to be cooperative. We have to let go of our fear of the truth and trust God to forgive us just as we are. Then we can begin to forgive ourselves and learn to relax in the shelter of God's grace.

Forgiveness of ourselves effectively dissolves many of our insecurities and self-deprecations. It allows us to let go of who we *were* in order to focus on who we *are* in Christ, and who we *are becoming.* That in turn will allow us to cease our critical judging. When we have effectively forgiven ourselves, we can be more accepting of the frailties of others, seeking to encourage and develop them rather than to criticize or fear what they represent.

Search me, Oh God, and know my heart; Try me and know my anxious thoughts; and see if there be any hurtful way in me, And lead me in the everlasting way.   (Psalm 139:23-24 NAS)

Forgiveness overcoming blame.

Most marital problems are rooted in unforgiveness of parents. We transfer onto our marriage partner the job of fulfilling needs that were unfulfilled by our parents. We misdirect our angers and accusations that truly belong against our parents towards our spouses.

For example, you may believe in your mind that you have forgiven your parents for their slowness or negligence in complimenting, affirming, or recognizing you as a child. But in your relationship with your spouse, you strongly demand constant presence and punctuality, undivided attention when you are talking, unfailing remembrance of anniversaries and birthdays, and that affections be expressed in just the right way.

This kind of behavior normally indicates lingering unforgiveness of parents who paid less attention to you than you needed. Disappointment and over-reacting when your spouse doesn't perform according to your expectations usually indicates long-standing insecurity about being loved by parents and siblings.

Inability or unwillingness to forgive also breeds unfaithfulness. Constantly focusing on hurts, frustrations, or disappointments about what we want from our spouse creates temptations to look for needs to be fulfilled by other persons outside the marriage.

This is especially insidious and deceptive in that we may be unaware of unfulfilled needs until someone else unexpectedly begins to fill them. We're caught off guard and into the beginning of an affair before we're aware.

When forgiveness is complete, we will find ourselves more at peace about what we did or did not receive in our childhood, and we will be delighted to discover ourselves to be more tolerant, understanding, and accepting of what our spouse and others are able to give to us.

Dear God, creator and giver of all that is good in life,

I don't want to hold anything in my heart and spirit which could block my relationship with You, or cause me to miss Your blessing or prevent me from becoming all You created me to be. I recognize I have often suppressed my feelings, not realizing they could fester and become poison to myself and others.

Sometimes I have denied my real responses, pretending that everything was okay when it wasn't. And many times I have held on to angers and nursed irritations, making up speeches because I thought I had a right to feel the way I did. I confess there are many unforgivenesses lodged in my heart. I don't know how to let them go, but I am choosing right now to forgive _____, for _____.

I trust You, Lord, to enter the depths of my heart by the door of my repeated choices, and make forgiveness real in me. Please forgive me for the ways my unforgivenesses have afflicted others and grieved Your heart. Enable me to identify compassionately with the pain others feel.

By Your grace I ask for a blessing of love and well-being for those who have injured me.

Amen

Life Application:
Facing Truth and Reality
Where We Are on the Journey Toward Forgiveness

1. Review the four levels of wounding that require forgiveness which are discussed in this chapter (See page 64). Which of these woundings can you identify as happening in your own life?

Identify below the kinds of "pain" you have experienced in each of these situations. Check these feelings against the kinds of responses you have made at this point in your life (See third column of the chart on page 64).

Bruise (Page 54) Friends & co-workers saying things like: I'm to fat, I need to do something with my hair, face, clothes I wear. To forgive them & ask God to help me not to be bitter towards them

Cut (Page 57) adopted parents saying: I'm worthless, won't amt to anything, I'm ugly, no man would ever want me. I forgive my adopted parents. I feel numb & some distrust. I don't know quite how to deal with this. I don't want to get sucked into her dark & painful world.

Open Wound (Page 59) Being told that I'll never amt to anything, because I'm stupid and that I'm ugly. I ...

Crippling Injury (Page 61) Being abducted & raped by several men & left for dead. Being abused by adopted has left bitterness in my heart with the male species. How do you forgive people you don't know

2. Uncovering incomplete forgiveness—
If there is a person in your life who has hurt you deeply at some time and you believe you have forgiven him/her, apply the six measures of determining whether unforgiveness is still lodged in your heart. (See pages 65-73)

Share this evaluation with a friend or with your group members. Identify below any clues you have discovered that indicate your forgiveness is not complete.

1) a little
2) a while
3) better understanding of those who hurt
4)

3. Review the section on the "importance of self forgiveness" and "forgiveness overcoming blame" (pages 73-74). In what ways do you recognize yourself in these descriptions? Pray for God's forgiveness and for your ability to achieve a greater degree of self-forgiveness.

Chapter Four

The Process of Forgiveness
Giving Feet to Our Good Intentions

No two days have ever been the same
Subtle though the difference.
The mark of change is sure.
And like the sun that creeps across
A new horizon with each dawn
Our transience brings a birthing
With the light of each new day.

A touch of joy and then of pain
A question asked, a lesson learned
A wonder freshly seen.
Each day is a passage
From place to place
Friend to friend
Life to life.

Knowing this, what then are we to do?
But cherish where we've been
As life's rare treasures
We carry on our way -
Work through the passages
With faith enough to conquer fear -
And like explorers who are always open
To the value of surprise
Greet our unseen future with a cheer!

Lee Bowman

Preparation for moving toward forgiveness.

C enturies ago, the prophet Jeremiah admonished the people that it was as difficult for them to escape their sin as it was for the leopard to change its spots. This wisdom applied to us today means that ingrained patterns of thought and behavior are difficult, if not impossible, to change by the efforts of our flesh. We shouldn't be surprised when our good intentions are not enough to overcome and reshape the deep issues of our heart.

The person who says, *"Forgiveness has always been easy for me because I'm just naturally a forgiving person,"* hasn't really entered into what unforgiveness is all about and has no awareness of what is lodged in his heart and spirit. Even with the grace of Jesus, achieving forgiveness is not easy. The reason forgiveness is so difficult is that whatever has become lodged in our heart and spirit is, indeed, stuck there.

Unforgiveness gets stuck in us like rust on an old iron frying pan.

Unforgiveness is comprised of hate, no matter how much we have euphemized. We hedge on our feelings by saying such things as: *"Well, I've forgiven him, but I don't have to like him; and besides, he did that on purpose!"* We hate people we blame for doing us wrong. Strikingly, we most often hate people who are closest to us. This doesn't mean we don't love them. We are ambivalent creatures; we can love the people we hate, and hate the people we love. Hate and love can live side by side in our hearts.

In reality, forgiveness is so difficult to accomplish because all our grudges are expressions of hate, given dwelling places in our heart. We don't like to think that we hate, but if we are not expressing love, we are really hating, and hate murders. Our grudges are sinful because grudges murder relationships between people and destroy God's purpose for us to live in unity. Grudges also are sin because they afflict the other person with energy that is spiritually wounding.

We know that we have passed from death to life, because we love our brothers. Anyone who does not love, remains in death. Anyone who hates his brother is a murderer, and you know that no murderer has eternal life in him.

(1 John 3:14-15)

According to Old Testament law there was no remission of sins and no forgiveness without the sacrificial shedding of blood in worship to God. In Saint Paul's letter to the Hebrew Christians, he reminded them of this fundamental requirement of the Mosaic law. However, Paul taught that the blood sacrifice, required by God's Law, was completely and everlastingly fulfilled through Jesus Christ, God's Son, who by dying on the cross became the sacrifice for all who would believe in Him and come repentantly before God for salvation.

> *Only through the blood of Jesus*
> *does God grant the power*
> *to cancel sin and grant forgiveness.*

That is the first and most important lesson to be learned about forgiveness.

In order for the power of Christ's forgiveness to work in us, we must make ourselves available in the following ways:

♦ **Believe that the Lord Jesus Christ has power to accomplish forgiveness in us, through us, for us.**

If we have trouble letting that belief really penetrate into the doubting recesses of our heart, we need to affirm the power of Jesus in us by praying in confidence again and again.

Lord, I believe that what You did on the cross is effective for me. I believe that You live in me. I believe that as You live in me, what I can't accomplish in my flesh, You can accomplish in me, through me, and for me. I can't do any more than choose to forgive. I don't know how to make anyone feel forgiven. I can't get it done, but I believe You can, and I trustingly give it up to You.

♦ **Be patient about what it will take to achieve forgiveness.**

Logic should tell us that if we spend a long time building up practices of unforgiveness, it may take a long time to disassemble those practices. When we realize that we have unforgiveness lodged in the heart, it is natural for us to want to go immediately to the cross, pray about it, and root out the unforgiveness so we can get on with our lives. We are conditioned by our society to expect fast communication, fast food, and fast travel. We want instant gratification for our desires.

But that may be too easy. It will take a lot of patience to learn to do things God's way rather than according to our own wishes. A quick fix of an unforgiving heart would not teach us to become sensitive to other people. We would not develop openness and the wise understandings that are so essential for the healing of broken relationships and the maintenance of those which have been restored. The healing is of God, but the lifestyle of forgiveness grows through our faithful discipline of letting Christ live in us.

> *Therefore as God's chosen people, holy and dearly loved, clothe yourselves with compassion, kindness, humility, gentleness, and patience. Bear with each other and forgive whatever grievances you may have against one another. And over all these virtues put on love, which binds them all together in perfect unity.*   *(Colossians 3:12-14)*

♦ **Prayerfully seek to become empathetic with those we perceive have wronged us.**

Because the Lord wants us to come into true healing, it is as if He says to us: *"You go through Gethsemane like I went through Gethsemane."* Let's consider what that means.

On the night in which Jesus was arrested and tried, He went with His disciples to Gethsemane, a garden area in the Kidran Valley below the Mount of Olives opposite Jerusalem. That night, in fervent prayer and anguish, Jesus struggled with and accepted the purpose of God—He would take upon Himself the burden of mankind's sins. He would drink the cup of wrath of the nations.

For thus the Lord, the God of Israel, says to me, "Take this cup of the wine of wrath from My hand, and cause all the nations, to whom I send you, to drink it. And they shall drink and stagger and go mad because of the sword that I will send among them." Then I took the cup from the Lord's hand, and made all the nations drink, to whom the Lord sent me.
(Jeremiah 25:15-17 NAS).

He would take into himself and become our sin. His struggle in the Garden of Gethsemane was *not* to accept having to die physically for us. He knew He had come from heaven to earth for that very purpose. But He had never been separated from His Father. Sin separates!

Who may ascend into the hill of the Lord? And who may stand on His holy place? He who has clean hands and a pure heart.
(Psalms 24:3-4)

That spiritual death of separation from His Father by becoming our sin, thus unable to stand in the holy place of His Father's presence, was why He cried out, *"Father, if Thou art willing, remove this cup from Me, not My will, but Thine be done."*

Becoming our sin, becoming one with us, was necessary to fulfill the law of God. The next day He would die as a sacrifice that we might be forgiven and brought back into right relationship with God. Therefore, in the intensity of that Gethsemane experience, Jesus went across time and space. He became us, in order to reap as us, and for us—the death on the cross we were due to reap because of our sin. Praying as the God-man, He identified with us, entered into us, and became our sin.

He made Him who knew no sin to be sin on our behalf, that we might become the righteousness of God in Him.
(2 Corinthians 5:21 NAS)

When we experience the Gethsemane prayer in relation to a person or situation that needs our forgiveness, we are saying to the Lord: *"Help me to empathize with him. Take me inside his heart.*

Let me feel his hurt, his fear, his doubt, his grief, his anger, his insecurity." Such an honest prayer is intended to open our minds and hearts to feel empathy with the very person who violated us. When we enter into oneness with Jesus as He identifies with the sin of the other, the lines that separate us get blurred.

- We lose the sense of us (the good guys) and them (the bad guys).
- We commence to change our attitude about being the wounded party, or the noble martyr.
- We start seeing what we may have done to cause the other to behave in hurtful ways.
- We begin to sense what vulnerability in us drew harm from the other person.
- We may also recognize how we both have been affected by the sin of all mankind.
- Our prayers change from *"Oh, God, help me forgive that dirty rascal who doesn't deserve it,"* to *"Oh, God, we are caught in sinful reactions. Forgive us! We stand at the foot of the cross, both of us sinners, crying out for mercy."*

Apply this to your marriage or to a close friendship. It seems to you that your partner is judgmental and continually wounds you with criticism. But when you enter into the Gethsemane prayer with Jesus, you enter into your partner's heart with empathy and understanding. You link that one's behavior with understanding of your own history and see that because of your response to those who have wounded you with criticism in the past, you have developed a pattern of actually drawing criticism out of others.

Your subtle behavior of withdrawal, defensiveness, or even callousness defiles the relationship with your partner and draws him/her into judgment and criticism of you. Understanding this will enable you to see the situation from the other person's perspective rather than only from your own. You can begin to respond in openness rather than blame.

♦ Repent of our own part in the subtle dynamics that cause relationships to be broken.

Freedom for us may come only when we learn to repent of those things in ourselves that draw people to hurt us.

> *Do not lie to one another, since you laid aside the old self with its evil practices, and have put on the new self, who is being renewed to a true knowledge according to the image of the One who created him.* *(Colossians 3:9-10 NAS)*

We lie to ourselves and to each other when we insist we are lily white and the other one, and only that one, is all wrong. With time, by the Gethsemane prayer and with growing insight, we can gain an understanding of ourselves and our enemies in new and more humble ways. We are not as innocent as we at first perceived ourselves to be. And those persons whom we first saw as the enemy are no longer perceived to be unfeeling monsters. They can be seen as they truly are—weak, needy, and insecure, just like us.

That is the secret. When we can get into the depths of our feelings and those of others, we lose our sense of isolation. Let's say it again for emphasis. Say it aloud as you read: *"We begin to feel at one with those who hurt us and cry out to God to forgive us OUR sin. We have sinned together."*

We must pray as in the Garden of Gethsemane, to give up our self-righteousness, break through our self-imposed isolation, and overcome false feelings of martyrdom. That is the price we must pay. We must recognize our own sin and repent of it. Recognition of sin and repentance breaks the cycle and begins to set us free.

This may sound like a lot of work, and it is. But we should remember that it is the Lord Jesus Christ through His Holy Spirit who gives us the power to move through the process of forgiving and to be made new in His likeness.

◆ Admit our own inadequacy to achieve forgiveness and humbly seek the Lord's help.

Like a child who is struggling unsuccessfully to pull a tight-fitting sweater off over his head, we may have to get to the point of crying out in frustration: *"Somebody please help me with this!"* We *can* overcome the old and be made new. The Lord expects us to become new creatures, living in forgiveness. He will equip us to do so if we come in repentance, asking for His help to overcome. He will free us of our old clothing of sin and clothe us anew in righteousness as we allow Him to live within us.

> *As God's chosen people, holy and dearly loved, clothe your-*
> *selves with compassion, kindness, humility, gentleness and*
> *patience. Bear with each other and forgive whatever griev-*
> *ances you may have against one another. Forgive as the Lord*
> *forgave you.*   *(Colossians 3: 12-13)*

Six steps to achieving forgiveness.

Ability to forgive is an individual matter, influenced by one's personality, temperament, social and cultural standards, spiritual maturity, readiness, and relationship with God. No formula can be used to guarantee success. However, in seeking to move through the process of forgiveness, we have found the following steps to be very important.

1. Honestly desire to become free of the burden of unfor-giveness and prepare to forgive.

No one can make you forgive, and forgiveness is not likely to happen if you are motivated only by feeling you "should" or "ought" to forgive. You must genuinely want to experience for-giveness. If possible, clearly identify what is causing your anger, disappointment, frustration, or hurt. Identify who and what it is that you need to forgive and be able to say openly and honestly, "*I choose to forgive.*"

Making such a choice may be very difficult, especially if the wound is fresh and the hurt is personal. Time helps to develop new perspectives, less clouded with emotion. Logic about the benefits of forgiveness will mellow the hurt. And oftentimes an ability to respond in humor will break through the heaviness and become therapeutic.

Our dear friend and fellow counselor Judy French tells of a time when she was ministering to a very angry young woman at a California family camp. The young woman's husband had left her to marry a Catholic nun. The young woman was embittered by the hurt and rejection and was at a seemingly impossible impasse about reconciling herself to the divorce. She refused to be comforted and choosing to forgive seemed totally out of the question.

"No, I can't forgive her!" she cried. *"What kind of a nun is she anyway, to take someone's husband?"*

Finally, Judy said to her, *"I don't think we can go any further. The only thing I can ask you to do is to pray for grace."*

She looked up at Judy, astonished, and cried out, *"That's her name! Her name is Grace!"*

At that, Judy couldn't contain herself and began to laugh openly. Then, the young woman started giggling and soon broke out in laughter too. That was the very thing she needed to tumble her walls of anger, come into the presence of the Lord, and let the Holy Spirit begin the process of forgiveness to accomplish healing in her life.

2. Sit down with a fair-minded counselor or friend and talk over the situation which requires forgiveness.

Don't attempt to be your own counselor because you probably will see the situation only from your point of view and in relationship to your own hurts or bitterness. Counseling will give you the perspective of another person and allow you to clarify and talk out your feelings.

The first to present his case seems right, till another comes forward and questions him.　　　　　*(Proverbs 18:17)*

Do not seek counsel from someone who obviously harbors grudges and judgments of his own. Choose a neutral person who has no stake in the situation that has caused the hurt. Choose a person who is a good listener, who is wise and will not make quick judgments.

A wise and fair-minded counselor or friend can perceive whether you are holding anger within or still have unresolved issues or bitter roots with which you need to deal. Be honest with your counselor. Listen and give serious thought to what he or she is saying. Then with the guidance of your counselor or friend, take the issue to the Lord in prayer.

3. Pray specifically about the person or situation that is the focus of a forgiveness issue.

Identify and clarify what it is you need to forgive. Verbalize your feelings and your desire to forgive. Say aloud in prayer, "*I forgive _____!*" Be specific and detailed. Be real! Believe it in prayer and expect the Lord to accomplish it as you continue to choose to forgive.

4. Do something to bless the one who is being forgiven.

Forgiveness is not a neutral act to be achieved only privately in the head and heart of the forgiver. To effectively free us from our burden, forgiveness must move from intellect to action. God's gracious gift of forgiveness is no gift at all if we quietly place it unopened on a shelf. To come into the fullness of its reconciling power, the gift of forgiveness must be unwrapped, cherished, and shared.

True forgiveness is demonstrated in our willingness to pray for and to facilitate good things happening in the life of the one who has hurt us. Without the outflowing of our blessing for the one who hurt us, we miss the point of our forgiveness and fall short of the blessing of grace which God has for us.

> . . . *all of you, live in harmony with one another; be sympathetic; love as brothers; be compassionate and humble.*
> *Do not repay evil with evil or insult with insult, but with blessing, because to this you were called so that you may inherit a blessing.*   *(1 Peter 3:8)*

Let's look closely at what the apostle Peter is saying here. He directs us to **Repay with BLESSING,** *because we are called to bless so that we may inherit a blessing!*

The very purpose of a Christian is to *bless* others. We are not to callously hold grudges, behave haughtily, or to repay evil with evil and insult with insult. It isn't enough to put unforgiveness to death. We must then pray blessing into the life of the person who hurt us. When we do that, we receive a blessing.

This principle is honored by God even on a national basis. After the defeat of Germany in World War I, France insisted that Germany be punished with burdensome reparations. These ultimately contributed to financial depression in Germany, social chaos, the rise of Nazi Germany, and the Second World War. Continuing unforgiveness against Germany blocked God's blessing from being realized and the entire European continent suffered the consequences.

After World War II, the people and the government of the United States pushed past the hurt and suffering of that cruel war and chose to bless its enemies. The people of Germany, Italy and Japan were not punished. Rather, they were given our hand of support and friendship in order to rebuild socially, economically, and politically, and to ensure future peace. Now Germany and Japan are strong economically, and two of our staunchest allies.

The United States received a blessing from that gracious act, and will continue to be blessed as long as it acts in humility and compassion and seeks to bless other nations in need. Nations and individuals who live without compassion and return evil for evil will write their own downfall.

Bless those who persecute you; bless and do not curse. Rejoice with those who rejoice; mourn with those who mourn. Live in harmony with one another. Do not be proud, but be willing to associate with people of low position. Do not be conceited.
Do not repay anyone evil for evil. Be careful to do what is right in the eyes of everybody. If it is possible, as far as it depends on you, live at peace with everyone.

(Romans 12: 14-18)

Continuing in this section of Scripture, Paul says:

Do not take revenge, my friends, but leave room for God's wrath, for it is written: "It is mine to revenge; I will repay," says the Lord. On the contrary, If your enemy is hungry, feed him; if he is thirsty, give him something to drink. In doing this, you will heap burning coals on his head. Do not be overcome with evil, but overcome evil with good.   (Romans 12: 19-21)

At first, this seems like a strange passage. We have heard a story from missionaries about how natives, when first exposed to this teaching, literally filled up containers with hot coals and dumped them on the heads of their enemies while they slept. The message here is more profound in its meaning and has been lost to our modern understanding.

In the time of the writing of this Scripture, people cooked over an open flame between two little bricks on the floor, using dried camel dung, water buffalo chips, or little twigs. Fuel was in short supply so nobody could keep a fire going all the time and starting a fire was not an easy task.

One person in the village was appointed to keep a small fire going all night. In the morning he would add fuel to make a larger fire and let it burn down to glowing coals. Then he would take a scoop, place the hot coals in a metal brazier on top of a wooden block on his head, and go around from kitchen to kitchen, using tongs to deliver hot coals between the bricks so the women in each family could start their own fires to prepare the morning meal.

This practice of heaping burning coals on someone's head gave birth to an idiomatic expression. To heap burning coals on someone's head is to turn him into a servant who brings the fire of love into the life and homes of others. Paul is saying that by returning good for evil and by blessing those who would hurt us, we turn the hurtful event around. They may be won over by our kindness and may become servants of God's grace.

For example, the seventh chapter of Acts records how the young Saul of Tarsus held the cloaks of the men who stoned Stephen to death. But Stephen prayed blessing for his persecutors and that act of returning good for evil was the beginning of what eventually resulted in Saul's becoming the great apostle Paul!

How are we to bless those who have hurt us? Start first by praying for them. Ask for God's will to be done in their life and for God's compassion, mercy, and grace to be with them. Then, seek to fulfill those admonitions clearly defined in Scripture:

♦ **Do not take revenge or repay evil for evil, but attempt to live in peace. If justice is due, leave it for the Lord to repay.** Obedience to this command might be as significant as refusing to retaliate with acts of violence, or choosing not to seek a punishing lawsuit. It might be as simple as choosing not to participate in gossip or to speak unkindly of the one who caused the hurt.

♦ **Attempt to be kind, understanding, and to live in harmony. Rejoice with those who rejoice and mourn with those who mourn.** Many hurtful situations begin because one or both parties in a relationship feel slighted when the other person has been insensitive or has failed to give the recognition and respect they believe they are due. Taking the time to notice other persons and to express a sincere interest in their successes and their sorrows rebuilds many bridges.

♦ **Put aside pride and conceit and be willing to associate with those you previously held in low esteem.** Simply assuming an attitude of non-judgment and being available for reestablishing relationships creates an environment in which blessings naturally can unfold. This is a primary purpose of the Gethsemane experience, to *"Be of the same mind toward one another, do not be haughty in mind, but associate with the lowly. Do not be wise in your own estimation."* (Romans 12:16) Or, we could translate that: *"do not be self-righteous in your own estimation"*—more righteous, that is, than that one who sinned against you.

♦ **Be available graciously to lend assistance in your enemy's time of need.** Take the opportunity to be encouraging and supportive. Actions speak more loudly than words. Kindness can break down long-standing walls.

> *But if your enemy is hungry, feed him, and if he is thirsty, give*
> *him a drink; for in doing so you will heap burning coals upon*
> *his head.*   *(Romans 12:20)*

5. Be prepared to suffer hurt to fulfill God's purpose.

Sometimes God cannot reach a person He wants to save because the person won't listen. God might then prompt the rebellious one to hurt a Christian in order to set in motion a chain of events that will demonstrate the power of God's love and draw the rebellious one into belief.

If a Christian is true to his calling, he will go into the Gethsemane prayer when he is persecuted or hurt, become one with the other, and through the process of forgiveness will begin blessing the one who hurt him. That act of forgiveness and subsequent blessing builds a bridge over which the love of God can flow into the rebellious person's heart.

Why do non-Christians persecute us? It may very well be that God is prompting them so that He may use that event to turn their hearts around, to bless them, and subsequently to bless others. This is why historically the blood of the martyrs has always been the seed of the church. God views this process of the Gethsemane prayer, forgiveness, and blessing as one of His most powerful evangelistic tools.

Thus it is that our suffering can be used for God's purposes. We are God's avenue of entrance to the hearts of His recalcitrant children. That is why we must hold fast to Christ our Lord and His example of forgiving love. We must forgive others their sins against us and pray for those who persecute and spitefully use us.

> *But in your hearts, set apart Christ as Lord. Always be pre-*
> *pared to give an answer to everyone who asks you to give a*
> *reason for the hope that you have. But do this with gentleness*
> *and respect, keeping a clear conscience, so that those who*
> *speak maliciously against your good behavior in Christ may*

be ashamed of their slander. It is better, if it is God's will, to suffer for doing good than for doing evil.   (1 Peter 3: 15-16)

Blessed are you when people insult you, persecute you and falsely say all kinds of evil against you because of Me. Rejoice and be glad, because great is your reward in heaven, for in the same way they persecuted the prophets who were before you.   (Matthew 5: 11-12)

Spend yourself in love for the person who hurt you. Christ's love in you will set you free. One of the primary purposes for the command to bless those who hurt us is to restore love in our hearts for them. This sets us free—and may be the Lord's way of causing that person to be healed and saved!

6. Seek reconciliation.

Reconciliation is that wonderful objective which completes the circle of forgiveness. People who have been separated by pride and sin move past their differences by forgiveness and blessing and come together in new understandings and restored relationships. Let us share how some dear friends have worked through a moving experience of forgiveness and reconciliation in their own lives.

Dick and Judy French are Elijah House Associates who operate a Christian counseling and retreat center in Parsons, Kansas, called the *Ministry of Reconciliation and Encouragement* (MORE). Dick found himself overwhelmingly disappointed, deeply hurt, and tremendously angry when his son, Kris, became involved with another woman and abandoned his wife and children. In the midst of Dick's emotional turmoil, the Lord spoke to him through James 5:16, as if to say, *"How can you possibly be a minister of love and restoration to others when you have so much unforgiveness lodged in your own heart? Take responsibility for your feelings and reactions, confess your sins, and be healed."*

Obediently, Dick went to a trusted friend who could be honest and lovingly confrontive with him. He repentantly confessed without making excuses and received assurance of forgiveness for his judgments against his son.

This experience proved to be very healing for Dick and allowed him to let go of his anger and disappointment by giving it up to the Lord. Dick was ready for reconciliation, but Kris was not. Caught up in his own anger, unforgiveness, and struggle with a drinking problem, Kris withdrew and refused to have any contact with his parents.

Dick and Judy were determined not to let their family crisis interfere with their ministry and they sought to be faithful to the Lord's calling in their lives. Their daily ministry went on, but for the next fifteen months they fervently prayed for the Lord to deal with Kris so that unity might be restored to the entire family.

A real crisis came for Kris when the state of Oklahoma cracked down on fathers who were behind in child support payments. Kris had been lax in his support, and when he was called into court the judge sternly gave him a four month jail sentence..

Even in jail, Kris still refused to receive mail, phone calls or visits from his parents. However, the Lord impressed upon Dick that he was to make the choice to forgive Kris and Lisa, the new woman in Kris' life, and go to the jail to see Kris. Dick marked a date and time on the calendar, three months from then, when the Lord impressed upon him to make the trip. When that day came, Dick set out for the jail in Tulsa, knowing that he was not included on the visitor's list of over 600 prisoners, and that he had little hope of being able to see his son.

That afternoon, as Dick stood in line to enter the detention center, he and Kris saw each other through the window. Kris mouthed the words, *"Get me out of here?"* Dick replied, mouthing the words, *"How can I? I didn't put you in there."* Then he added, *"I love you! I'm praying for you, son!"*

In jail, the Lord had been dealing with Kris to penetrate his hardness of heart. Hearing his father's words, Kris motioned for Dick to turn around, and when he did, he saw Lisa standing in line just four people behind him. Dick went outside to wait for Lisa and when she came out he said to her, *"There are a lot of complications in all this mess, but I want you to know that I forgive you, that I no longer hold anything against you, and that I will continue to pray for you and for the whole situation."*

That encounter at the jail, and Dick's choice to repent of his own judgments and forgive, provided the basis for communication, reconciliation, and healing which is happening in the entire family now. Kris and Lisa have come into a new and open relationship with Dick and Judy and with the Lord, even to the point of wanting this story to be shared as an encouragement for others to seek forgiveness and reconciliation.

We are moved by the beauty, pathos, and truth in Jesus' story of the Prodigal Son. We grieve over our own prodigal relationships and wish that somehow reconciliation could always be the happy ending toward which our life moves.

Some Christian apologists say that forgiveness is never complete until reconciliation is achieved. Others argue that in the realities of human relationships, full reconciliation may be unachievable and often not even desired.

Time and circumstances change us. We cannot experience the anguish of betrayal and the pain of alienation and remain the same persons we were. Nor can we expect the other persons to remain unchanged. Trauma makes us different.

Realistically speaking, reconciliation is never solely to return to the way things used to be. Reconciliation brings with it new perimeters of knowledge, understanding, and feelings.

If we have forgiven another person and sincerely want that person back in our life, we must realistically ask a series of questions:

- Between the fragmenting of our relationship and our coming into forgiveness, what has happened to each of us?
- Does the other person want reconciliation? Has that person moved on to new commitments and new relationships?
- Will the re-establishment of intimacy be constructive or destructive in the other's life or in our own?

If too much water has passed under the bridge, we may have to adjust to what is now possible—or impossible—between two people who are quite different than they used to be. A love may become a friendship. A dear friend may become no more than an acquaintance. Forgiveness may heal anger and bitterness, but realistically may have to fall short of reconciliation or even of establishing a friendly relationship. Such adjustments may be less than what we want and may carry pains and griefs of their own—but moving toward the freedom of forgiveness is worth the very best we have to give.

 Lord Jesus Christ,

We bless and praise You for your wisdom and Your grace. You have shown us how important it is to forgive—revealing that we must sow forgiveness in our lives, or we will reap the dreadful consequences of our sins of unforgiveness.

So often we have failed to accomplish forgiveness on our own, despite our good intentions and our striving, But through your grace, You have given us the power to succeed in spite of ourselves.

We thank You, Lord, that You came, and on the cross You said "It is finished." You took away the weight of our sin and our inability to forgive, and You died with them. Your death is our death. Your freedom is our freedom. Your life is our life.

We pray that we will learn with renewed hearts and minds how to trust You with our lives. Show us the places where we still hold grudges, where we are still angry. Show us how to walk through the process of forgiveness with You and be free.

Amen

Life Application:

The Process of Forgiveness
Giving Feet to Our Good Intentions

Making application of this chapter to your life is not merely a thought process—it will require an action plan to achieve forgiveness where unforgiven issues continue to burden you or cause you continuing alienation from others.

Select an unforgiveness issue in your life. In a notebook, make a list of specific actions you can take in each area below.

Be specific. Set a date and time to take action. Detail your plan. Carry out your plan and keep a journal of your progress and your feelings about what is happening.

1. Identify who and what it is you want to forgive. Be specific.

2. Talk over the situation with a fair-minded friend or counselor. (Set a date and time to do this and follow through.)

3. Pray specifically about the person or situation. Repentantly confess your role in the alienation and ask for God's guidance and wisdom. Ask for the Holy Spirit to achieve forgiveness within you.

4. Do something to bless the one who has been forgiven. Don't just pray blessing, take a specific action.

5. Be prepared to suffer hurt or continuing rejection. Think through an appropriate response ahead of time in order to be prepared. Be patient and give the process time.

6. Seek reconciliation with the offending party.
- Is this desirable?
- Is this reasonable?
- Is this possible?

Chapter Five

Forgiveness as a Lifestyle
Overcoming Life's Bitter Roots

୶

*Look long
In the mirror of your mind
When happy moments falter
And like a flickering candle
Cease to give an even light.*

*Consider your ways
When privileged gifts
Are redefined as rights,
When hard-won friendships
Are no longer given tender care,
When family members are treated as enemies
And togetherness becomes a waste of time,
When compassion can be postponed
Until convenient,
And God has been reduced to cosmic mind.*

*Consider your ways
Because ingratitude is a disease,
Bitterness cripples,
And callousness kills.
Unforgiveness is a dark cloud
That blots out the sun
And God can make life a symphony
Only for those who are thankful daily
And have the will to live in love.*

Lee Bowman

F orgiveness is refreshment for our spirits. It is the essential lifestyle of Christians who are serious about faithfully following the commands of the Lord Jesus Christ. However, many people view forgiveness begrudgingly as a duty that occasionally must be extended to someone who has done us dirty. We really don't want to think of forgiveness as a way of life to be lived in every moment and in every relationship.

Coming into the lifestyle of forgiveness is not easy. It is a process which begins with our will to forgive and is brought to completion through the power of Jesus Christ who alone can work the necessary transformation in us.

In many ways we can compare the process of forgiveness to a skill which must be learned and practiced until it becomes as automatic as breathing. Think for a moment of what it takes to become competent on snow skis. Skiing requires mastery of fundamentals and considerable practice to combine balance, coordination, agility, and speed into a safe and exhilarating run down a mountain slope. Similarly, playing a musical instrument requires learning to handle the instrument properly, and spending many hours in practice to develop even a semblance of artistry. Skiing and performing on a musical instrument are skills which are wonderfully enriching. They are skills which can be learned, enjoyed, and put to good use. However, they are not skills essential to productive living.

Forgiveness is a necessary skill,
an essential ingredient
for living a productive life.

To the degree in which it affects who we are and how we relate to others in our world, the skill of forgiveness is more like walking, talking, and eating. We can do without skiing, and without being able to make music. But if we don't learn how to walk, talk, or eat, how can we survive? If we don't learn the skill of forgiveness and practice it diligently, until we develop mastery over every wounding, we become severely crippled in our ability to relate to others and to live in harmony in our world.

Perhaps the most evident sign of holding unforgiveness in our hearts is the way we sometimes attack other people when we are wronged and become irritated. If the heart is full of unforgiveness, that's what naturally will be reflected in our speech. Look at what Jesus said:

> . . . *For out of the overflow of the heart the mouth speaks. The good man brings good things out of the good stored up in him, and the evil man brings evil out of the evil stored up in him.*
> *(Matthew 12:34-35)*

It's not acceptable to unstop what is in our hearts, run off at the mouth, and pour untempered negative feelings on others whenever we're stimulated. God will hold us accountable for all that we say and do. Forgiveness is necessary.

> *But I tell you that men will have to give account on the day of judgment for every careless word they have spoken.*
> *(Matthew 12:36)*

We are not talking about suppressing feelings. Legitimate feelings should be expressed. We need to become aware of the vast difference between *rehearsing* feelings and attitudes, and *confessing* them. We are in constant relationship with people who stimulate us—often to anger and hurt. In the name of honesty and in an attempt to defuse our angers, we can go around spilling all that is in our hearts—thinking that speaking feelings is the same as dealing with them. But without repentance and willingness to give our angers to Jesus to be put to death on the cross, what we actually are doing is continually *rehearsing* our negative feelings.

***When we rehearse our grievances,
they become more and more ingrained in us
and will become permanently
lodged in our heart.***

If we are truly willing to deal with our issues and give our angers and bitternesses to Jesus to be dealt death blows, then what comes from our mouths will be *confession.*

Jesus accomplishes forgiveness in us, but we must first repentantly confess our feelings and seek to forgive as a daily, moment-by-moment discipline. This must be practiced repeatedly, continuously, so that our hearts are softened and our negative feelings become malleable to change. This opens us to receive the grace of Jesus Christ and leads to release and healing.

Paul encouraged those in the church at Ephesus to put their quarreling aside and to adopt the forgiving nature of God:

> *Let all bitterness and wrath and anger and clamor and slander be put away from you, along with all malice. And be kind to one another, tender-hearted, forgiving each other, just as God in Christ also has forgiven you.   (Ephesians 4: 31-32 NAS)*

In James we also find this sound advice:

> *Everyone should be quick to listen, slow to speak and slow to become angry, for man's anger does not bring about the righteous life that God desires.   (James 1: 19-20)*

> *If anyone considers himself religious and yet does not keep a tight rein on his tongue, he deceives himself and his religion is worthless.   (James 1:26)*

> *With it* (the tongue) *we bless our Lord and Father; and with it we curse men, who have been made in the likeness of God; from the same mouth come both blessing and cursing. My brethren, these things ought not to be this way.*
>
> *(James 3: 9-10 NAS)*

We have to be aware that we must stop our untempered speech at the very beginning because once a harsh, angry, or false word is spoken, the whole stream comes out. An ancient Proverb says this in a very graphic way:

> *The beginning of strife is like letting out water, so abandon the quarrel before it breaks out.* *(Proverbs 17:14 NAS)*

The Bible can be very down to earth—no one can stop once he begins to pee! The proverb means that once you begin to unleash your emotions in quarreling and strife, you'll not be able to stop until it's all said and done. It warns that we have to practice a daily discipline of not letting ourselves speak in anger or bitterness, because once we speak it we are into strife. We stimulate each other with negative feelings which invariably result in hassles that destroy us and the people we love.

> *What causes fights and quarrels among you? Don't they come from your desires that battle within you? You want something but don't get it. You kill and covet, but you cannot have what you want. You quarrel and fight. You do not have, because you do not ask God.* *(James 4:1-2)*

Hurt by those we know the best.

It is easier to take criticism from a stranger than it is from someone we love. With strangers, we tend to play down the value of the comments, or dismiss complaints as being "their problem." We can ignore their criticisms and walk away from the situation without being seriously affected. On the other hand, the primary people in our lives have great capacity to hook into us and trigger passionate unleashing of our emotions. We react with more volatility to those we know and love because we care more about what they think and how they treat us. We have higher expectations of them to deal with us fairly and with kindness.

For example, if someone you hardly know insults you, how long does it take you to get over it? Most people say *"A moment or two." "A quick prayer." "It's done in a few seconds."* But if your wife or husband, or father or mother, says exactly the same thing to you, how long does it take you to get over it? Some people have groaned and said, "*A lifetime!*" Others have said, "*A long time, because it really hurts!*"

Consider the impact these comments can have when they come from someone you love and live with:

- You *never* listen to me. You *never* hear a word I say!
- You *always* criticize!
- You *never* think how that might make me feel!
- You're a failure as a mother!
- Why can't you keep this house neat? (When you live in a
- very small house with half a dozen children)

So we see that a word carelessly spoken by a loved one hurts. We begin to think: "*What are they questioning? My worth? My performance? The love I have poured out? The years of service I have given? The sacrificial consideration I have given?*"

Very quickly we can be undone! In our anger and hurt we begin to rehearse catalogs of how we have been treated unfairly. We lash out in anger to counter the injustice we feel.

- You don't do so good yourself.
- I don't see you doing much to help.
- You could:
  Carry a few dirty dishes to the kitchen
  Not drop your dirty clothes wherever you take them off
  Not leave newspapers strewn around the room
  Clean up the messes you make
  Supervise the kids once in a while
  Give me a break!

Angry reactions stimulate counter reactions and quarrels erupt. Continually rehearsing hurts turns them into bitterness, and our unforgiveness becomes lodged in the heart.

To avoid this, we must check what is in our heart and with the Lord's help, deal with our issues of unforgiveness at their root— through short, immediate, "flash prayers." This does not mean we should deny our feelings or suppress them. Rather, we should seek to understand why we feel the way we do, put our feelings in perspective to see how unbridled emotions can hurt us and others, and seek the Lord's help in coming into real forgiveness. This will have to be done momentarily, every day, as a lifestyle of prayer and forgiveness.

Recognizing our false sense of forgiveness.

The mystery of unforgiveness is that most Christians know they should be forgiving, but understand very little how forgiveness is really accomplished. What typically happens is that when we experience a hurt, we attempt to handle the need to forgive by simply repressing our feelings. Or, we attempt to deal with serious matters of the heart by handling them mentally. Feelings are thus denied, rationalized away, or simply shoved down inside.

Or, we go through the motions of praying forgiveness on the surface, unaware that our heart hasn't been in it and that forgiveness hasn't really happened.

This is the reason so many of us wind up fighting battles with each other and within ourselves. Our true feelings are neither defined nor dealt with. We think we have accomplished forgiveness, but we have mostly suppressed feelings in an attempt to "be Christian." In reality, suppression of feelings avoids dealing with them and creates a false sense of being a forgiving person. Then when the pressure of so many pent-up feelings becomes too great, an explosion of emotion erupts and our stored-up suppressed hostility comes spilling out.

Repression of feelings can often result in tragedy in the home. It is not uncommon for staunch Christian parents, who are rigidly focused on uncompromisingly appropriate behavior, to be radically intolerant of the natural expression of feelings their children have. Although these parents maintain controlled demeanors of gentility to the outside world, their angers and intolerance are suppressed to the point of extreme frustration by which violence erupts in the home. They explode into frequent outbursts of verbal abuse, abusive spanking, and setting of rigid rules to enforce behavior. The hypocrisy between public appearances and actual at-home behavior destroys trust, causes confusion, and fosters rebellion in the children. The structure of the entire family is put in jeopardy.

Only by going through a daily discipline of honestly acknowl-edging feelings, choosing to forgive, and coming repentantly to the Lord for help can forgiveness become a healthy lifestyle skill.

Daily discipline of forgiveness prayer.

Discipline means consistency—consistency of staying in touch with our feelings of hurt, disappointment, rejection, and bitterness as they come up moment-by-moment each day. Individual hurts may seem like tiny barbs we can pass off by saying they don't really bother us. But when we get a whole pin cushion full of needles, we start experiencing physical and emotional pain and discomfort that makes life miserable. The most healthy thing we can do is to hon-estly admit feelings and seek a way to constructively remove those painful barbs through forgiveness.

A daily habit of prayer is the most effective way to do this. De-veloping a habit of prayer doesn't mean we have to retreat into solitude and fervent supplication on our knees every time a negative feeling pops up, or every time someone says something hurtful to us. We can stay tuned in through "flash prayers"—instant turnings to God for immediate morsels of understanding, guidance, courage, wisdom, and release.

When a loved one says something hurtful that angers us, we can deal constructively with our feelings through a flash prayer, some-what like the following, silently delivered to God:

Lord those words hurt me and I'm angry. Please help me un-derstand why they were said. I repent of the role I may have played in causing this outburst. Put my negative feelings to death through the power of Your cross, and enable me to live in Your pure love and forgiveness.

Flash prayers allow us to admit our feelings,
repent of our sinful responses,
submit ourselves to God's ability to accomplish forgiveness
in us, and move on to live in the freedom
and refreshment of God's grace.

Prayer is communication to and from God. Our prayers don't have to be pretty or formal. They can be a mere few words spoken in the midst of our confusion and delivered up silently in our minds. God asks only for honesty and the desire to come into relationship with Him.

The value of flash prayers is that they deal *immediately* with our needs. They save us from stockpiling our feelings, falsely massaging our situation until we can make sense of it, or taking fleshly control through our own strength and knowledge. We get ourselves into trouble when we postpone coming to God with our pain. He is the only one who can truly heal us. When we postpone coming to Him, we condemn ourselves to failure by trying to do it all on our own. The Lord has asked us to come to Him when we are weak and burdened, and He has promised us that He will give us rest.

> *Humble yourselves, therefore, under the mighty hand of God, that He may exalt you at the proper time, casting all your anxiety upon Him, because He cares for you.*
> *(1 Peter 5:6-7 NAS)*

How should we pray? We should pray simply, honestly, and continually. We should establish a habit of prayer so that moment-by-moment we live in a discipline of forgiveness that becomes a lifestyle.

> *Be joyful always, pray continually, give thanks in all circumstances, for this is God's will for you in Christ Jesus.*
> *(1 Thessalonians 5:16-18)*

Unforgiveness at the root of our nature.

Forgiveness becomes most difficult to achieve when a pervading attitude of unforgiveness exists because it is at the root of one's nature—when it has become built in (oftentimes unknowingly) as a practice of life. Paul describes this in his letteer to the Hebrews as a "bitter root" which has the capacity to defile others by its lack of grace.

See to it that no one misses the grace of God and that no bitter root grows up to cause trouble and defile many.
(Hebrews 12:15 NAS)

Unfortunately, many people do not understand what a "root" is in our spiritual and emotional makeup.

A "root" is a hidden practiced way
of drinking nurture or unnurture,
from God, others, ourselves, and nature.

Consider how the root of a tree functions. A tree is much more than what we see above the ground. It sends roots deep into the soil of its environment to drink nourishment. If the soil is good, the root system is healthy and strong and the tree flourishes. Healthy roots enable a tree to hold firm to the supporting soil in stormy weather and give the tree resiliency to stay healthy in times of draught.

If the soil is bad, the root system will be weakened, causing the tree to languish or to fall. Without a good root system a tree can easily be destroyed by disease or storms and does not have the capacity to thrive in times of stress.

In Austin, Texas, there was an ancient oak tree called the Treaty Oak near the state capital. It had been the site of many historic meetings in pioneer days and was much revered by the citizens of Texas. Several years ago, in an act of malicious revenge spawned by bitterness over a lost state agency job, a man poured herbicide on the ground around the base of the Treaty Oak. Despite desperate attempts by state botanists to treat the tree and purge the soil of poison, the root system drank the toxic chemicals and the Treaty Oak began to die.

We drink nurture and harm from the soil of our environment in a similar way. A "root" is the way we reach into others through our spirits, and through the structures we have built, to drink either life or that which destroys life. Because we are mixed vessels, we do both.

Roots developed in earliest childhood become the nurturing patterns which shape our character development. For example, a child who lives with parents who never give him affection and continually shove him aside is likely to develop that style of relationship as his own root behavior. If we have not been lovingly and attentively nurtured, we will not have practiced habits of reaching into and expecting nurture from others. Rather, we will develop "bitter roots" which are practiced habits of not giving or expecting to receive nurture. Such bitter roots can cause the "heart of stone" referred to in Ezekiel. Healing requires that the bitter root be taken out—a wonder of transformation accomplished through the power of God.

I will give you a new heart and put a new spirit within you; and I will remove the heart of stone from your flesh and give you a heart of flesh. (Ezekiel 36:26)

What we experience in life, particularly in early childhood, imprints attitudinal and behavioral patterns in us so subtle we may be completely unaware why we think and behave the way we do. Our bitter roots may seem completely normal to us—until we come into experiences in which our life patterns conflict with those of other persons.

This is especially true when we get married and are called on to relate to our spouse in a level of intimacy never experienced before. If we have a bitter root of never learning how to drink nurture from another person, then we will not know how to receive nurture even when it is lovingly offered, or know how to give it. We will avoid intimacy, withhold affection, and not recognize sincere caring when our spouse reaches out to us. We will expect rejection, coldness and manipulation. We will be suspicious or perhaps cynical about expressions of affection. Thus our bitter roots spring up to defile the marital relationship and the entire family structure.

Our bitter root structure can be so deep and so hidden that we are not even aware of its presence. Yet, we continually drink harm that can negatively impact the lives of those around us and eventually destroy us. Every one of us has hundreds of bitter roots which affect our attitudes and behavior.

Drinking harm or drinking nurture.

How do we drink harm from God?
◆ By falsely projecting onto Him the unwholesome images and negative expectations we have developed through our experiences with our natural fathers and other authority figures. That false god, created from our misconceptions and judgmental responses to woundings, will inevitably poison our lives and the lives of others around us.

With the pure Thou dost show Thyself pure; and with the crooked Thou dost show Thyself twisted.   (Psalms 18:26 NAS)

How do we drink nurture from God?
◆ By faithfully and thoughtfully grounding our root structure in the true and loving Father God, revealed to us in Scripture and in the person of the Lord Jesus Christ.
◆ By letting Him love us through His presence in corporate worship and private devotions! We can only do this if our root system is trained to do it by our relationship with our parents. Only a good tree can produce good fruit.

How do we drink harm from ourselves?
◆ By drinking from the accumulation of unhealed wounds, unrepented judgments and negative expectations in the storehouse of our hearts.

How do we drink nurture from ourselves?
◆ By drawing from the treasure of blessings we have received.

- By recalling and celebrating the good times we have en-joyed with parents and family friends.
- By recounting the valuable lessons learned as we struggled through difficult situations, and by praising God for it all.
- By remembering the times when all seemed hopeless, and celebrating the fact that we are no longer in that state.
- By choosing to know our integrity in Christ and stand in it no matter what the world thinks of us.
- By celebrating our identity and belonging as beloved children of God—apart from performance—whether we feel His love or not.

"Jesus loves me! this I know, for the Bible tells me so;
 Little ones to Him belong; they are weak but He is strong.
Jesus loves me! He who died, heaven's gates to open wide!
 He will wash away my sin, let this little child come in.
Jesus loves me! loves me still, tho I'm very weak and ill;
 From His shining throne on high, comes to watch me where I lie.
Jesus loves me! He will stay close beside me all the way;
 If I love Him when I die, He will take me home on high."
Anna B. Warner, 1860

Dear Lord,

Forgiveness isn't easy. I've made so many choices to forgive, and just about the time I think I've finally achieved forgiveness, something happens to upset me again. How long is it going to take?

You said I would have to walk in a moment-by-moment discipline of forgiveness before it could become a way of life in me. But I'm discouraged, especially when I don't see any real change in the people I'm forgiving.

Oh, oh! I'm sorry Lord. I'm rehearsing my negative feelings again. And forgiving others isn't supposed to change them. It changes me.

Soften my heart. Enable me to receive Your grace and healing in such a way that my heart's desire is to extend Your quality of grace and love to others for their sake, not just for mine.

And thanks for the reminder, Lord, that You have forgiven me again and again although I haven't done anything to deserve it.

Amen

Life Application:

Forgiveness as a Lifestyle
Overcoming Life's Bitter Roots

1. What is your personal pattern of handling stressful and/or hurtful situations? Do you express your emotions openly and try to forgive immediately, or do you tend to hold emotions inside and brood about hurtful situations? Do you hold a lot of old resentments inside? Rate yourself on the following scale from one to five:

Open expression of feelings and immediate for- giveness				Holding feel- ings inside and brooding over hurts
1	2	3	4	5

2. What is the difference between *confessing* feelings and *rehearsing* them (Review pages 101-102)? Write out your definition of these concepts below:
   Confessing:

   Rehearsing:

3. Can you identify any deeply held hurts that you have been holding inside for a number of years—perhaps even from your childhood—that you have been unwilling or unable to forgive and release? What bad fruit in your life might be traceable to those unforgivenesses? Write out a list of those situations so you can identify areas of prayer needed to deal with root causes.

4. When we encounter situations that are hurtful or that bring up painful old memories, we seldom have time immediately to enter into solitude and prayer to deal with the feelings. However, we can pray "flash prayers" silently at these times to help us cope and to keep feelings from festering into bitterness (See pages 104-105).

In the space below, construct for yourself a carefully thought out "flash prayer" that you can lift up to God at times when stressful and hurtful situations come up during your day.

5. Much of our troubles seem bigger than they really are because we have not practiced a pattern of self-nurture. Review the list of ways we can drink nurture from ourselves on page 110-111. Then, write a letter to a friend. In the letter, refrain from mentioning the troubles you may be having right now. Rather, utilize this catalog of self-nurturing ideas to testify to the positive view you can take of your life.

Chapter Six

Balance through Forgiveness
Unity in Primary Relationships

LIVING A BALANCED LIFE IS TO:
Tell the truth
Be transparent, open, straight on
Look directly into people's eyes
Touch without fear
Give lovingly and accept gratefully
Let go when experiencing trust
Be strong when trusted
Linger over goodness
Move on when it is time
Listen without restlessness
Disagree pleasantly
Live without bitterness
Be OK when saying Yes
Feel OK when saying No
Have joy in other's success
Encourage others to fly
Make decisions with clarity
Admit wrongs openly
Demand quality
Live expectantly
Look inward for security
And above all else,
FORGIVE.

Lee Bowman

Basic principles of walking daily in forgiveness can be applied to every area of our lives. In this chapter we will be focusing mainly on relationships within marriage. But we would like for you to interpolate what we say here to all other interpersonal relationships as well. The same dynamics happen between employee and employer, brother and sister, pastor and congregation, and between friends. Principles of forgiveness apply any time we enter into day-by-day relationships.

We have been fortunate that in all our years of marriage we have never lost the spark of romance and have a very blessed relationship. From what we have already shared, you know that is something of a miracle. But we want you to understand that the miraculous relationship we have is not something that just happened to us—it took a lot of work and much turning to the Lord for wisdom, strength, and guidance.

Marriage is a special kind of relationship. It is more than just love or friendship. When a couple marries, they become one flesh.

Wives, submit to your husbands as to the Lord. For the husband is the head of the wife as Christ is the head of the church, His body, of which He is the Savior. Now as the church submits to Christ, so also wives should submit to their husbands in everything.

Husbands, love your wives, just as Christ loved the church and gave Himself up for her to make her holy, cleansing her by the washing with water through the word, and to present her to Himself as a radiant church, without stain or wrinkle or any other blemish, but holy and blameless. In this same way, husbands ought to love their wives as their own bodies. He who loves his wife loves himself. After all, no one ever hated his own body but he feeds and cares for it, just as Christ does the church for we are members of His body. For this reason a man will leave his father and mother and be united to his wife, and the two will become one flesh.

(Ephesians 5:22-31)

St. Paul has often received "bad press" as a woman-hater because he taught that women should be subject to their husbands. But note here that he is writing to husbands and wives, saying that they should be subject to one another. Nowhere in the history of the world until that time had anyone taught that men should be subject to their wives! This is a recurring theme with Paul.

> *The husband should give to his wife her conjugal rights, and likewise the wife to her husband. For the wife does not rule over her own body, but the husband does; likewise the husband does not rule over his own body, but the wife does.*
> *(1 Corinthians 7:3-4 RSV)*

Paul was no woman-hater. When he said that husbands and wives should be mutually subject to one another in love and respect, he was a revolutionary advocate of the liberation of women.

This love and respect is to be accomplished out of reverence to Christ, an important principle for us to remember. To the degree that each of us is subject to Jesus Christ, the Lord enables us to relate to each other in mutual love and respect. The reverse corollary is also true. To the degree we are *not* subject to Jesus Christ, He will not rule our hearts, and forgiveness will not be built into us as a moment-by-moment daily practice. When we do not submit our wills to Him, He will not empower us to live with others in unity and forgiveness. We *will* be subject to one another, but to each other's selfish flesh rather than blessing.

Good, bad, or indifferent, each of us does relate to every person with whom we come in contact. We affect others in some way, both individually and corporately. In that sense, we cannot avoid being subject to each other. Without the presence of Jesus in our lives, we will relate to others only according to the flesh and not in the Spirit. Only when the cross is present is the redeeming grace of Jesus Christ able to transform our relationships to produce blessing rather than harm.

That's why we have so many broken relationships and divorces today. People are paying lip service to Jesus but they don't know how to walk with Him moment-by-moment. They can't stay in long-term relationships because the fire of unforgiveness burns within them.

When a man and woman enter the marriage relationship, the husband and wife often tend to counter-balance each other. For example, if one tends to talk too much, the other is likely to remain silent. If one is a strong disciplinarian, the other probably will be more lax. When this tendency to counter-balance one another occurs, tensions develop between partners because one or the other is pressed to lean uncomfortably toward behavior contrary to his or her normal temperament or beliefs. The same dynamic is also true between siblings, friends, or business associates who work closely together.

The key to overcoming this dynamic is in the sensitive application of the cross and forgiveness. We must evaluate what is happening in the relationship and put our own ego in proper perspective. Then, moment-by-moment, day-by-day, we can take the selfish practices of our relationships to the cross and ease the tensions through forgiveness so that through the power of Jesus Christ our selfishness can be put to death and our wounded feelings healed.

If anyone would come after me, he must deny himself and take up his cross and follow me. *(Matthew 16:24)*

Balancing relationships through forgiveness.

🐝 *Paula: One plus one is more than two.*

The Lord has made us in a very fearful and wonderful way. Quite a few years ago I had an auto accident in which I sustained an injury to my back. I don't understand everything about the bone and muscle structure of the back, but to put it simply, the doctor told me that the injury would cause me some temporary trouble in moving my left leg. However, he said not to worry, because in time the other muscles and nerves would take over and my leg movement would be restored.

The doctor was right; it happened just as he said it would. I came to understand with awe and wonder how when certain parts lose their capacity to function properly, the Lord has so built us that another part of our body takes over to compensate. This is also evident when blind persons develop heightened senses of touch and smell.

Applying this to our "one flesh" relationship in a marriage, it means that when one part of John's capacity to function is somehow crippled, at some point I naturally take over to compensate for what he is not able to do. This is because I am part of him and I feel it. My compensation may be unconscious and completely automatic, but it is real. The Lord made us that way for blessing, so that we can be effective as a unit together.

> *Two are better than one, because they have a good return for their work: If one falls down, his friend can help him up. But pity the man who falls and has no one to help him up! Also, if two lie down together, they will keep warm. But how can one keep warm alone? Though one may be overpowered, two can defend themselves. A cord of three strands is not quickly broken.* (Ecclesiastes 4:9-12)

The corporateness within the Body of Christ allows a similar balancing effect to take place. When one of us is weakened or incapacitated, somebody else is there with God-given ability to take over and compensate for the other. But this natural compensation can cause friction between those involved. Sometimes our taking over to compensate for the another's weakness tends to put the other person down, resulting in their hurt or bitterness. Or, we may become angry when we are thrust into a position in which we have to compensate for the other person. We resent being put there. Or, perhaps the other person's inability forces us to do something we don't want to do, or goes against our nature.

We may not be happy about it, but there we are. That's what corporateness creates. We have to learn to accept the other person, forgive, and minister to him or her. We have to learn to submit everything to the Lord Jesus so there can be balance without strain, without judgment, without accusation, without bitterness, and without resentment.

🍎 ***Paula:*** *Achieving balance in relationships.*

Our struggle to achieve balanced relationships is much like playing on a teeter-totter. I remember as a little girl going to the playground and getting up on the teeter-totter with a friend. Sometimes my playmate would be much larger than I and the unbalanced weight would cause his end to go clear to the ground, leaving me stranded way up in the air. I would bounce frantically to make my end come down. We both wanted to have a good time going up and down and up and down. Both of us were supposed to enjoy it but we couldn't. The balance was just too far off.

In our immaturity we'd start yelling at each other. We'd say *"You're too big,"* or, *"You're not playing fair and I'm not having any fun,"* both trying hard to make it work but blaming the other person.

Then maybe a big brother or a dad would come along. Taking pity on us, he would get up on the middle of the teeter-totter and stand on the board, straddling the fulcrum, exerting the power of his muscles to shift the balance back and forth to allow us to go up and down with fun. We didn't have to wait until we had grown to the same size to put ourselves in balance. That big brother or Dad supplied it. He maintained what we couldn't achieve.

The Lord Jesus Christ is our big brother in all relationships. We don't have to demand that the other back off or back down. We don't have to insist that the other person change in any way. We just accept and embrace the other person as he is right now—love him where he is, and give the difference to the Lord Jesus Christ. To achieve balance through forgiveness in our relationships, we must begin by inviting Jesus moment-by-moment to be that dynamic power of love in our lives.

🍎 *Paula: Achieving balance in parenting.*

In John's and my relationship, the issue of how to discipline our children was one of the most difficult things to give to the Lord for establishing balance. By his nature John always wanted to think issues through. When one of the children would get into trouble, John would resist leaping in immediately to administer discipline. He wanted to mull things over—to think about the situation slowly. He wanted to refine and polish his thinking and decide logically, calmly, and coolly what he was going to do. He and I grew up in big families, so it wasn't just that there were a lot of children around needing quick action, or that we weren't used to the constant needs of children.

Because John liked to carefully think over how to handle issues of discipline, he would often withdraw inside himself when troubles arose. Later, he would come out to do something about it.

The way I was raised in my family, parents were much more likely to jump in quickly to express an opinion or settle a dispute. Discipline was swift. When my father was absent and my mother was too busy to notice what my younger brothers were doing, I felt like I had to leap in to discipline them or I would be run over by the mob. There was something in me that needed to control and manage in order to defend myself. I realize now there was unforgiveness behind my need for control.

Later in life as a young mother, I had not yet really forgiven the rambunctiousness of my brothers. Consequently, my impatience and driving need to discipline my own children was based in unforgiveness of my brothers. It was also fueled by my anger at John for not disciplining as quickly as I thought he should, and for sometimes being preoccupied and unaware of the children's behavior.

On the other hand, John's mother characteristically jumped in too quickly to discipline—oftentimes harshly and unfairly. John's father was normally very good and fair with discipline, but he would prefer to think a situation over thoroughly beforehand. Oftentimes John's mother would push his father to jump in immediately, and the subsequent discipline would be corrupted by her quick judgments rather than his own wisdom. The result was often harsh and unfair, nobody being happy. John became determined to be like his Dad and not like his mother. Behind that was judgment of his parents, and consequent abiding unforgiveness.

These kinds of reactions are built into all our root systems. In our marital relationships, we develop patterns of struggling to balance each other's flesh. I would often discipline the children with impatience, angry at John for not being right there on the spot to handle the situation for me. I really had not given him the opportunity to be there to handle it his own way, yet I would blame him for not being there in the way I wanted him to be.

When I would try to restrain myself from jumping in too soon, I would inevitably find it necessary to remind John that disciplinary action needed to be taken. I tried to program him into doing it, and not always very quietly. You can imagine what impact that had on John and on the children.

John tried to get in there and perform his duties more quickly. But sometimes he had stored up so much of what he was mulling over to polish and perfect, that when I would push him he would passionately explode and react toward the children in an out-of-balance way. Then, when I would see that the situation was out-of-balance, I would leap in and say, "No, John! No, not that way!"

I remember one experience that our poor son Loren had to live through. Loren really did need a lot of discipline. He was the kind of kid who would look you right in the eye and say *"No!"* and if you spanked him for something, he would stoically reply, *"That didn't hurt!"* What do you do? You don't want to beat your child, but there he was standing unrepentantly, defiantly saying *"that didn't hurt."* He was tremendously gutsy.

🍎 *John . . .* I think Loren had been in a long spell of this kind of behavior and I was fed up with it. Paula had been pushing me all along with comments like, *"John, we're going to have to do something about Loren—we can't let him go on like this."*

Finally, one day I exploded and said, *"Loren, you are going to learn to obey! Whether or not you see any reason for it, you are going to do what you are told!"* So I got a little jar of dried beans, dumped them in the kitchen floor and told Loren that as an act of obedience, he was to push each of those beans across the kitchen floor with his nose! (I'm ashamed of that today, but in the heat of the moment it seemed to make sense.)

🍎 *Paula . . .* There Loren was, a poor little kid down on his knees. Under great duress he began pushing beans across the floor with his nose. I was a distraught mother who all the time had been nagging my husband with, *"You've got to do something drastic to get this kid into shape."* Now I was saying, *"Oh, John, please, not this! You are going too far!"* The necessity for forgiveness was all intertwined in us. Everybody had to forgive everybody, and there was no easy way to do it. (Thank God, that experience taught John more than it did Loren; he never tried anything like that again.)

When another one of our sons was in his teenage "individuation process," it was very difficult to break through his sullen barrier to obtain any kind of information or even to have a decent conversation. In my impatience, again I pushed John, saying, *"Your son is being very difficult and you are going to have to have a talk with him."* (Notice—the teenager had now ceased to be *our* son and had become *your* son.)

John would sit there quietly mulling over how he would approach this kid. Then when I would really hold the torch to John to get him to do something against his nature, he would explode emotionally at me and at our son. You can imagine how effective that was in promoting better communication!

We had to forgive. We had to undergo a round of forgive-nesses, calling on the Lord to provide the balance for us. Until that point, we had not grown adequately in the Lord to really under-stand what was going on or how to stop ourselves in the midst of unbalanced situations. We had to call on the Lord, repent, and for-give each other.

Jesus will corral our sinful nature if we are walking with Him and ask His forgiveness for the off-balance things we have done. That's the real key. I had to quit praying earnestly, *"Lord, get John's attention! Lord, change John! Lord, make John aware! Lord, cause him to be there when the kids need discipline!"*

By the power of the Lord, I had to arrive at complete forgive-ness of John and of myself before Jesus could really take over and be the balance between us.

It is still hard for John to confront. It remains too easy for me to express my opinion in some situations. I'll be nice in public, but at home I can express my opinions quickly and loudly. Jesus is the one who can and will hold the balance if we ask Him to.

❧ *John* . . . In trying to strike a balance in the way Paula and I disciplined our children, I knew we were going to have to go to the Lord for help. Unfortunately, my initial prayers were misdirected and ineffective. I would pray fervently, *"Oh, Lord, if you would just calm Paula down, I could handle discipline in my own way. Please give her the patience not to jump in and take control of the prob-lem."*

> **We can't expect Christ to intervene**
> **when we pray**
> **confessing another person's sin.**

It took me quite a while to realize that my prayers were not being answered because I was praying wrongfully. I was trying to make the Lord change Paula without accepting responsibility for my own role. Only when I became repentant for my own actions and began to pray for my own forgiveness and my own inability to adjust did the situation begin to change for the better between us.

A more enlightened prayer eventually became, *"Lord, I repent that I jeopardized Paula in that way. I repent of my abdication of responsibility which induced her to jump in and take charge. Forgive me for my insensitivity and help me to assume a properly active and decisive role in disciplining the children."*

The point is, we must confess our own sin and be willing to do whatever is necessary to set things straight.

❧ *John: Accepting personal accountability.*

I have to confess that the issue of discipline was not the only area of tension in our family. There were other behaviors I had to take responsibility for in order to come to a place of forgiveness and death of self within the family.

As a youth, I was destined to be a prophet—with all the gifts and none of the wisdom! Therefore I was a mystical dreamer, frequently drifting off into my own imaginative world. For example, my family would send me upstairs to get something and I'd not only forget what it was I was to get, I'd forget I was sent! They'd have to send someone to retrieve both me and what I was supposed to find.

At dinner I would start thinking and dreaming about what someone had said. Meanwhile, the conversation would switch to several other topics. When I finally figured out the first topic, I would interject a comment. Everyone laughed and said, *"Where were you, John, having your quiet time? We quit talking about that five minutes ago."*

Later in life when I was in the pastorate, Paula and I liked to make calls on people as a couple. Because I was a dreamer, I developed a pattern of letting Paula do all the talking. I'd sit there sensing where people were and analyzing and thinking. Because my mind was drifting I would lose the turn of the conversation. When I would finally come around and make a comment, it often came from way out in left field.

Before we would go to visit, Paula would say, *"John, as the pastor you've got to meet people where they are. You've got to visit with people and really listen. It hurts them when you're in a dream world and don't communicate."*

So I would be determined to do better and really visit with people. But when I fell silent for a few moments, Paula would get nervous and jump in to take over the conversation. I'd get interested in some point and lose the drift of the conversation. Then when I'd come back in and say something, as usual it would be off the subject and inappropriate, and Paula would wish I hadn't said anything at all!

That pattern didn't stop when I prayed, *"Lord, will you make Paula give me a chance to talk. Just corral her, Lord."*

Only when I repented of my part and brought my dreamy nature to death on the cross could I begin to really be there and to stay tuned in to the conversation. I had to pray that the Lord might bring me out to be more present. I had jeopardized Paula, making her feel overly responsible to visit with the people.

When we counter-balance and drive each other to unhappy positions, we'll not accomplish anything by appealing to God to change the other person. We have to be willing to change ourselves by confession and repentance.

❧ *Paula* . . . As a child I was extremely shy. It was against my nature to make conversations with people. At home it was easy enough for me to be open and talkative, but meeting new people and taking the lead in conversations in public had always been difficult. But in pastoral ministry together, I felt the need so deeply to balance what John was not doing that I had to thrust myself into conversations that were really stressful for me.

I felt resentment at being forced into that kind of position. It was of my own choosing, of course, and John was not deliberately causing me hurt or discomfort. Nevertheless, my hostility continued toward him. What he could not or would not do was causing me to stretch beyond my comfort zone. As part of my praying I had to repent of that resentment and hostility. I had to thank the Lord for using this kind of an uncomfortable situation to force me to come out of myself to meet people. And I had to ask for the Lord's help to change my pattern of judging John and pushing him to be different—into a pattern of acceptance and encouragement.

❦ *John* . . . What we are saying is that any time God unites a couple, He brings together people who are perfectly designed to grind against each other. We don't usually perceive the grinding as blessing but it is. Our grinding against each other becomes blessing when the balancing power of Christ is there at the center of our living to bring us to personal repentance, death of self, and forgiveness of each other. The prayer from our hearts should be, *"Lord, forgive me!"* That's forgive *me*, not forgive *her* (or *him*).

❦ *Paula: Letting go and trusting in each other.*

Another difficult area lay in our attitudes toward adventure and spontaneity. I remember as a child doing adventurous things. I often chose to skate down a steep hill in front of our house, or climb high up in a tall tree. I enjoyed feeling adventurous. But that was all under my control. Adventure was okay if I were choosing to do it.

I think that tendency to control was in me from the very beginning of life. My in utero and birth experience was as dangerous as jumping off a cliff because my mother had a ruptured appendix shortly after her marriage and had been advised by the doctor to postpone having children for several years. When she became pregnant with me, the fact that I was developing in her womb endangered her life. There was a lot of fear, tension, and anxiety as I was born. Insecurity as a baby resulted in frequent and prolonged crying my mother didn't know how to handle.

As a very small child I opened the door to the laundry chute and fell down the chute head first. Fortunately I landed in a basket full of clothes rather than the concrete basement floor. But as a child I remember that fear of leaping into something because there was terror of letting go and losing control.

As a young woman, I came into relationship with John and he didn't have that kind of cautious fear in him. He seldom stopped to count the danger or the cost. He was always ready to plow right in to adventure.

When we were in seminary in Chicago and would go to Lake Michigan for a picnic, John and my brother Jerry would jump into the lake and begin swimming straight out from shore until we couldn't see them any more. When John would return after my long period of anxiety, I would angrily remind him, *"You are my husband, the only one I have. These are your small children. You are the only father they have."*

When I came to the point of forgiving him for not taking thought, his heart became able to hear. Then the Lord prompted him to swim along the shore line instead of out of sight (from 57th Street to 87th Street).

Many years later when we moved to Idaho it was a terror for me to ride in a car with John on snow-covered roads in the mountains. If I were driving the car I wasn't that afraid. I was in control. I had practiced into myself, *"I will put one foot in front of the other, and I will overcome the thing that causes me fear."* I can remember, in every area of my life, facing my fears and difficult things by consciously choosing to risk. The Lord honored that and empowered me to overcome many fears. But I could not seem to trust when things were out of my control in the hands of other people.

When John was driving, I constantly found myself gripping the arm rests with white knuckles. *"John, for goodness' sake, please slow down."*

This became a real issue. I experienced a lot of resentment because he would so often say, *"Get hold of yourself, Paula. Just decide you're going to get over it!"*

On snow-covered mountain roads, I would nag, *"Slow down, John!"* He'd reply, *"We're only going 20 miles per hour!"* And I would say, *"Well, slow down!"*

I would nag until finally John would say, *"Shut your eyes and shut your mouth. Just lie back and pray in the Spirit."*

That was effective, but still it seemed like he was being very unfair and insensitive, just telling me to get over it. That's what I'd been doing all my life—getting over my fears by just taking it and bullying my way through. I wanted John to undergird, strengthen, comfort and reassure me—not just say, *"You're on your own, kid, now just do something about it."* I was angry at him and my anger didn't do anything but reinforce his response.

I had to come to the point of forgiving all the way back to the beginning—forgiving the people, the circumstances, and God for everything I had reacted to that had instilled insecurity and fear in me. I had to ask forgiveness for building all those defenses. I asked the Lord to break up the dry and resistant soil of my past experiences—to prepare me to be more receptive to the new seeds of adventure He wanted to plant within me. The Lord is in process of doing that still today!

🐛 *John* . . . I had to come to see that I was not in fact so courageous as I had thought. The Lord revealed there had been much to fear in my childhood, and I had overcompensated by reckless courage. The real root of my courage was actually fear. When I was able to acknowledge that in myself, I could be compassionate in regard to Paula's fears rather than contemptuous. I no longer had to compulsively take chances just to prove my manhood. The key was death of self, forgiveness of those who had frightened me, and surrender of my self to the Lord's kind of courage. Then I could ask forgiveness of Paula.

🐛 *John: Celebrating our uniqueness.*
Although I was always the adventurous one, I also perceived myself to be the logical one. Everything had to have a reason. I would frequently say, *"Now Paula, what's your reason? What's your starting point? Where do you plan to come out?"*

Paula wasn't made like that. You should see the way the house got painted. I'd come in the door and find Paula painting a room. A squiggle of paint here and a squiggle of paint there. I'd say, *"What are you doing?"* And she would reply, *"I'm painting the room."*

It was obvious to me that anyone with logic started in the upper left hand corner of one wall and painted across and down, and so proceeded around the room. But to Paula, that was boring!

🐛 *Paula* . . . It seemed logical to me that when you have a pan of latex paint and a roller, you don't have to get stuck in boring ways. You can take liberties and express your creativity because no matter where you start, the paint blends in. I'm an artist, so I'd put on some music and make lovely patterns all over the walls, and then fill in the spaces. That was fun! And it seemed plenty logical to me!

🍎 *John* . . . You should see the way we paint the walls these days. Paula makes designs all over, and fills them in. I paint the trim at the ceiling, floor and windows. This is a way of saying that when forgiveness becomes a daily practice, our differences become the spice of life and we can have fun rather then be threatened.

You can see the kind of dynamic we were always in. We had to quit judging each other as being right or wrong. We had to choose to accept the other one in the midst of diversity.

Forgiveness has to happen on a daily and hourly basis. When we do that, life becomes a blessing. An ancient sage once said that if two people always agree, one of them is unnecessary. Our differences in life become blessings when the cross and the blood of Jesus Christ are at the center, and we can forgive each other through His intercession about the ways in which we are different. The grace of God's forgiveness releases us to be forgiving and we don't have to be afraid of our differences any more.

🍎 *John: From push-pull to balance.*

In our marriage relationship, I was the mystical one, always out there searching for some new and wonderful thing in the Lord—having mountaintop experiences and sailing off into the heavens. That meant I was out there having all kinds of experiences while the kingdom at home was marked by skid marks—Paula's. She would frequently say, *"We're not going down another blind alley, are we, John?"*

Of course, the more Paula didn't understand my searches and remonstrated against them, the more I was determined to launch into them. And so, the more I'd be out there frantically trying to find reality and discover new things, the more she'd react—leaving black skid marks all along the road of our history!

Dynamics of this kind are bound to happen in any relationship, especially in marriage. We pull back and forth against each other, struggling to overcome resistances and to put limits on the other's perceived excesses. Balance lies in forgiving and calling on Christ through the power of the cross to bring our own selves to death—and since we're stubborn—calling on Him to intercede for us moment by moment.

> *He who searches the hearts knows what the mind of the Spirit is, because He intercedes for the saints according to the will of God.* *(Romans 8:27)*

Renouncing our need to make demands on those persons we love.

> *If anyone comes to me and does not hate his father and mother, his wife and children, his brothers and sisters—yes, even his own life—he cannot be my disciple.* *(Luke 14:26)*

These words raise an important issue, difficult to understand. Jesus was asking for undivided devotion from His disciples. He knew they would have to cut themselves free from the demands other relationships would make on them. Of course our Lord would never call us to hate wrongly. We use words in many ways. I love God, my wife, my dog, and a good hamburger, all differently. Just so, the word hate has different levels and different meanings.

Our father and mother, wife and children, brothers and sisters, race, nationality, culture, school, church, and friends can be viewed as a womb in which our character was formed. All were saturated through with sin, and so in many ways we reacted and were formed in sinful ways. When we are born anew, it is like being born out of that sinful womb. If we don't turn and cut the umbilical cord, the old blood of the old life flows into the new and spoils it.

Practically, this means that when we are born anew in Christ, we must cut free from all the old ways of relating so that we can be formed anew solely by the Holy Spirit in Christ. To do that, we must "hate" the continuing carnal influence of all those that formed us and choose only the Lord and His way to reform us. (More on this need to be cut free can be found in our book *Restoring the Christian Family*, chapter 18, entitled "Renunciation, or Cutting Free.")

In our humanity, we press others to obtain what we want and need, and we are pressed by others to give what they want and need. There is a world of demand coming from and foisted upon each of us.

> *All unregenerate love is use,*
> *exploitation, manipulation, possession,*
> *control and demand.*

We learned how to love in the world before we came to Jesus. All our ways of loving are filled with the world's ways of demanding and controlling, measuring, judging and manipulating others to fulfill what we want.

🍓 *John: Unspoken demands controlling our responses to each other.*

Living with Paula, I was not free to be who I am because there was a world of demand coming across from her flesh saying I had to be a certain way for her. Living with me, she was not free to be who she is because there was a subconscious world of demand coming from me. We would say to each other in subtle ways *"If you love me you are going to act the way I expect you to act. If you don't act this way, you don't love me and I need love."*

After a hard day at work, I'd drive home thinking I would come in and give Paula a big hug and visit with her. But the moment I'd come through the door, I could sense demand coming from her which said, *"You come in here and talk with me!"* The demand took away the gift. It immediately dampened my desire to visit with her. I reacted with quiet reserve, choosing not to communicate as I had planned.

🍂 *Paula*... I'd been thinking all day that I would like to greet John warmly with a big hug, but then give him time to collect himself. I planned to bring him a glass of iced tea and let him settle down and be himself without making demands when he comes in. But the moment John came through the door I sensed a demand that said, *"Just let me alone. Get out of my face. Don't ask me to do anything!"* His demand prevented my giving him a gift of quiet solitude. I would begin to think angrily, *"He should realize I've had a tough day, too, and I have a need for communication with him that deserves to be fulfilled."*

🍂 *John*... This world of demand is built into all of us. And sometimes our demands are not subconscious or even subtle. We can make very conscious strident demands. If our demands are not satisfied, we can feel disappointed, deserted and even betrayed. When we receive Jesus into our lives, we need to renounce and bring to death that entire world of demand. Paula and I never fell out of love with one another, but when we came to understand these internal demands, each of us said, *"In Jesus name, I renounce my love for you."*

That may sound strange—that we should renounce our love for each other! But what we were renouncing was our fleshly way of loving which places unreasonable demands on the other person. The Lord quickly resurrected His kind of love in us for each other. Human love imprisons. The Lord's love in us sets others free.

Opposing poles of demand such as this operate unconsciously between married couples, family members, and co-workers all the time. Unspoken expectations are passed back and forth and we respond in ways difficult to analyze or even to understand. Our unconscious demands, even those growing out of sincere love, erect barriers which keep others off balance and keep us from freely giving and receiving through God's grace.

What we need to do after we receive Jesus into our lives is to pray *"Lord, let my entire world of demand come to death. I renounce my love that places demands on others."*

God is still in the love business, so when we do this, the love of Jesus through us will set the other person free to be who he or she is. Because of demands born out of our own needs, our unregenerate love imprisons others. When we renounce unregenerate love, the love of God fills us and sets the other person free. The cross and forgiveness are central because we must bring to death all the worldly ways we've learned to love and to demand love from each other. When our own demanding love is dealt a death blow, the love of Christ can flow through us to the other person in a free and undemanding way. Jesus said:

> *I tell you the truth, unless a kernel of wheat falls to the ground and dies, it remains only a single seed. But if it dies, it produces many seeds. The man who loves his life will lose it, while the man who hates his life in this world will keep it for eternal life. Whoever serves me must follow me; and where I am, my servant will also be. My Father will honor the one who serves me.*   *(John 12:24-25)*

Until we die to our self-centered selfish way of loving, we are in fact trying to control everyone and everything around. People don't want to be controlled. They resent being reduced to satellites in our orbit. Consequently, our selfish love isolates us. We remain alone and the fullness of life is lost to us. I used to say to Paula, *"You've got a carousel going. There's only one place for me to jump on, and if I don't get on there you think I don't love you!"* Now I'm free to be myself, knowing she'll choose me and love me.

If our self-serving way of loving is brought to death on the cross, we radiate a warm and nurturing environment characteristic of the nature of Christ. Others then feel free to be themselves around us, and free to respond to us in trust and love. Thus, through death to our selves, we gain a life of fruitful relationships.

Reverence for Christ in our lives.

We need to understand fully what reverence for Christ means. Christ came and gave His life in order that we might be set free—in order that we might become who we were created to be, and in order that we might not have to remain in bondage to sin.

To have reverence for Christ means to allow Him access within us to accomplish effectively everything for which He died on the cross. That means we need to submit to Him all of our feelings, our past, our present, our daily irritations, our demanding attitudes, our manipulations, and our unforgivenesses. We have to give all of this to Christ that He might effectively bring these things to death on the cross, that He might live in us fully.

I have been crucified with Christ; and it is no longer I who live, but Christ lives in me; and the life which I now live in the flesh I now live by faith in the Son of God, who loved me, and delivered Himself up for me. *(Galatians 2:20 NAS)*

Now those who belong to Christ Jesus have crucified the flesh with its passions and desires. *(Galatians 5:24 NAS)*

If we allow Jesus full access to our entire being to accomplish within us what He came to do, then we can be subject to our partners or our friends in blessed relationships. Otherwise, we will be subject to every unregenerate thing within ourselves and others, and we will experience an unending series of struggles, striving, unforgivenesses, and pain.

Jesus did a finished work
in our salvation by dying on the cross.
But we must respond by incorporating
His grace into our reborn life.

Death to self, rebirth to love others to life.

We have witnessed a number of situations in which people have worked out this wonder of death, rebirth, and forgiveness in their lives. One of these was a young woman who was an active member of our church but at that time her husband was not at all involved in church activities. She prayerfully sought God's will for how she might better relate to her husband so that he might more fully share in her faith. The Lord's message to her heart was to back off from many church activities because she needed to meet her husband where he was, that he might able to draw closer to where she was.

> *Wives, . . . be submissive to your husbands so that, if any of them do not believe the word, they may be won over without words by the behavior of their wives, when they see the purity and reverence of your lives.* *(1 Peter 3:1-2)*

She determined to do this by limiting her church activities just to Sunday morning worship for a while and by staying home to devote special attention to her husband to deepen their relationship. She took care to express herself to him with renewed affection and to give of her time and energy to be a good wife and homemaker. This new focus of her time and attention soon began to melt his heart. It wasn't long before he began to be won over to the Christian faith she professed. The Lord enabled him to identify the grace she was sharing and the love she was giving as coming from God and His people.

Her husband became active in the church and grew so quickly that he soon surpassed his wife in spiritual depth, maturity, and ability to serve the Lord. At first, this angered her, and she complained to us, *"After all the time I spent learning and growing in the Lord, how is it that he can come to the Lord and so quickly race right on past me in Christian growth?"* The Lord then prompted her to realize that her husband's spiritual growth was what she had been praying for all along. All the grace that had poured into her life had spread through her into him. Also, she realized the Scripture tells us that the unbelieving partner is sanctified through the believing partner.

For the unbelieving husband has been sanctified through his wife, and the unbelieving wife has been sanctified through her believing husband. *(1 Corinthians 7:14)*

She had chosen to honor her husband with renewed intimacy and devotion, and it had released the grace that was already upon him. We need to know that our prayers will be hindered if we pray for somebody with judgment, blame, and unforgiveness in our hearts. This housewife had chosen to forgive, to let the Lord cleanse her heart, and to love her husband unconditionally. Because of this, her prayers were empowered and effective in winning him.

She realized that in spirit her husband had been participating in everything she had been learning because he was one flesh with her. It was only that his spiritual growth had not yet come to a conscious level. It hadn't begun to be worked out in his life. But he had been drinking in blessing at deep levels through who and what she was. Her forgiveness and her laying down of her life for him enabled all of that to take root. It gave him the power to choose and to stand for Jesus Christ on his own.

Forgiveness and regenerate love work the other way too, for husbands who pray that their wives might come into relationship with the Lord.

Husbands, in the same way be considerate as you live with your wives, and treat them with respect as the weaker partner and as heirs with you of the gracious gift of life, so that nothing will hinder your prayers. *(1 Peter 3:7)*

When one partner comes to the Lord before the other, it is not a sign that the one who becomes a believer first is more spiritual. If it happens that a wife comes to the Lord before the husband, this does not mean she should assume leadership as the head of the family until the husband becomes a believer. It is the husband's role to be the head of the family whether or not he has accepted Christ as his Savior. The wife should support and encourage her husband and set an example of Christian love and grace for him. A Christian husband should do the same for his wife.

God's truth revealed in a fairy tale.

Fairy tales live on through history because they reveal truths about human interactions. Our need to work out love and forgiveness is beautifully allegorized in the fairy tale of Hansel and Gretel and the Snow Queen.

Hansel and Gretel were brother and sister who enjoyed life together. One day while flying in her chariot, the wicked Snow Queen hurled a dart of ice into Hansel's heart, swooped down, and carried him away.

Gretel went through all kinds of perils trying to find her brother Hansel. When she finally found him and began to draw near, he was not happy to see her, and drew away. The closer she got to him the meaner he became. Whenever Gretel came close, her love was like warm fire that threatened to melt the ice thorn which had developed a life of its own and hung on tenaciously to keep from losing its power. At last, her love melted the ice thorn, it fell out and Hansel returned to himself—and to Gretel.

That kind of dynamic often happens between married couples. When one partner comes into a life-changing experience with the Lord and becomes more loving, the other partner may at first fail to rejoice in the experience. As that new kind of love begins to be expressed by one toward the other, it's an unsettling experience. The warmth of the new love is a threat to the frozen heart. Vulnerability is frightening and often causes the partner to withdraw or act with hostility. Why? Because the warmth of love and deeper intimacy melts the heart of stone, the other is afraid and knows he will have to change. To resist the threat of change, we often choose to hurt the other person in order to keep the fire at a safe distance.

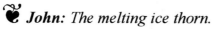 *John: The melting ice thorn.*

I used to do this with Paula. We'd have a wonderful time together in prayer, in sharing, in teaching, and in bed. Then within about two or three days I would find myself doing something mean to her. The reason is that her warmth and love were getting too close to my heart of stone—she was melting my ice thorn. That was making me uncomfortably vulnerable. There was hurt in my heart from unforgiveness toward my mother. I dared not allow myself to enter too deeply into trust with a woman. Because Paula was getting too close to me, my castle was being threatened. Therefore, I unconsciously sabotaged our intimacy.

Tension between sin and spiritual healing.

In our conscious mind we don't want to admit there's anything we haven't faced or gained mastery over. We don't want to be threatened by thoughts of our own weaknesses and sins, hostilities and unforgivenesses. We want to feel that we're in control.

Our mind is like a container that stores various thought processes. At the top is the conscious level where we actively deal with issues of life and interact with others in relationships. The conscious level represents perhaps only 20 percent of what our mental container holds. The other 80 percent is on a subconscious level—still within us but suppressed so as not to clog our thinking or throw us into mental overload.

However, we run into difficulty when we confront problems or sin issues which we have not reconciled or adequately processed on a concious level. We tend to shove those painful issues down into the subconscious mind, pretend they're not there, and put up a front of having it together and being in charge of our lives. Out of fear, insecurity, unforgiveness, or whatever other reason, we clamp the lid on our mental container and try to keep those problem issues from surfacing to a conscious level.

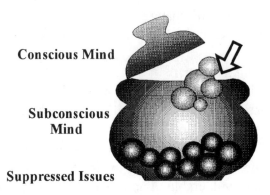

Conscious Mind

Subconscious Mind

Suppressed Issues

We push down problem issues we don't want to face, or don't want to admit are even there.

We cannot comfortably keep sin issues contained in our subconscious mind because our spirit yearns to be clean. Constant tension results. Through dreams or sudden insights, our spirit begins to push up each of those suppressed issues. Our conscious mind continues to shove them back under, not wanting to deal with them.

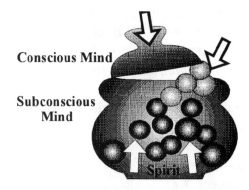

Conscious Mind

Subconscious Mind

Spirit

As we push issues down to be buried in the subconscious, our spirit pushes issues up to be healed. So, the war begins!

As long as we battle solely within our own conscious mind, uninfluenced by others, we can somewhat successfully keep the lid pressed down and continue to shut down the emergence of unsettled issues. We can maintain appearances of peace to the outside world. But if the purity of someone's love or the presence of the Holy Spirit becomes powerful enough, we no longer can suppress problem issues and they begin to boil around within us, threatening to explode irresistibly to the surface.

Isn't this true of many people you know? The face they wear for the outside world encourages you to believe they have it all together, but you can look into their eyes and know they have a lot of unresolved issues. They've won the battle of suppression they should not have won. Instead of openly dealing with issues that enslave them, they've shut everything down and live in false and troubled peace.

> *And they have healed the brokenness of My people superficially, saying, 'Peace, peace,' but there is no peace. . .*
> *(Jeremiah 6:14 NAS)*

Let someone like this encounter the love of a spouse, a brother or sister, or the moving presence of the Holy Spirit, and you have a surge of power which penetrates into the depths of the spirit. That power pushes up to consciousness each of those hidden things which have been suppressed within their mental container. This kind of love won't be denied, so the embattled soul erupts.

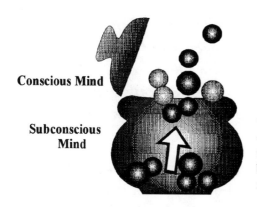

Conscious Mind

Subconscious Mind

When the Holy Spirit acts with power on someone's life, the suppressed trouble issues begin to be forced to the surface, resulting in emotional turmoil.

Unresolved issues of sin stirred up by the Holy Spirit.

Psychiatrists have told us that after a successful evangelistic crusade in a community (in which the power of the Holy Spirit is at work in the lives of many people), their offices are filled with counselees. Why? Because the power of God's love through the Holy Spirit has flooded deeply into people, stirring up sin issues they have long suppressed, so that great battling takes place.

The same is true within the Body of the Church. After the Holy Spirit moves in great waves within a church, you will often see eruptions of strife and dissensions among the members. Why? Because we have not fully understood how the Holy Spirit works. A major function of the Holy Spirit is to convict us of sin. The Holy Spirit empowers the inner being to bring up suppressed sins so they can be dealt with. Because people don't want to admit they have unresolved sin issues, they go into denial, project their turmoil outward, and fight with other people instead of facing the real issues.

This is a part of what Jesus meant when he said:

> *Do not suppose that I have come to bring peace to the earth. I did not come to bring peace, but a sword.*   *(Matthew 10:34)*

When the Lord enters our lives, He begins to stir us up because He wants to cleanse our hearts. He wants to purge the sin from our lives. We would like to think that since the Holy Spirit is present in our lives, we must be all right and we can expect only happiness and peace. It's just the other way around.

The Holy Spirit brings turmoil
as He convicts us of sin.
Peace comes as we learn to repent,
submit ourselves to God's will,
and thus begin to manifest fruits of the Spirit.

Actually it is not the Holy Spirit who brings turmoil, but our rebellious reactions to His cleansing fire. The Holy Spirit is interested first in the condition of our souls, not in the present state of our superficial happiness or contentment. He wants the deep wounds of our souls healed.

To understand this dynamic, it all boils down to one thing. After enjoying a good honeymoon time with one's spouse, or experiencing warm vulnerability with friends, or having spiritual growth in the church, we can expect trouble. The reason is not a bad reason. It isn't the devil attacking (although he may make use of this vulnerable time if we don't understand the dynamic). The painful stirring is from the Holy Spirit's bringing our sinful flesh up to consciousness to be dealt with.

Don't be disappointed if you have wonderful experiences in your prayer meeting only to find that the next time you are at each other's throats. You're probably grinding against each other because the Holy Spirit has done His job in bringing up issues you've been unwilling to face. The key is to resist the temptation to submerge them once again, or to project blame on others. Be honest with yourself. Search your soul for your own transgressions and take them to the Lord in repentance. Ask forgiveness and lay yourself open to live in a spirit of forgiveness toward others.

Often when a time of love and intimacy is followed by meanness or hostility directed at us, we take it personally as attack. This most often is not the case. We need to look beyond the superficial to understand what may in fact be happening.

🍎 *John: Learning to recognize the Holy Spirit at work.*

When I would withdraw after a time of special intimacy by being mean to Paula, she used to take it personally. She'd think, *"What did I do to deserve this?"* The fact is, she didn't do anything wrong. She did something wonderfully right. My meanness resulted from that in me which was threatened by the love which was growing between us. It was melting more of my stone-cold heart, and I was afraid.

Coming to understand this, Paula learned not to take my behavior personally but to be at peace within herself, to help me to understand what was happening, and to allow the Holy Spirit time to deal with me. The Holy Spirit then taught her to strengthen my spirit through prayer so I could maintain in vulnerable times, without having to flee.

> *I pray that out of His glorious riches He may strengthen you with power through His Spirit in your inner being, so that Christ may dwell in your hearts.*   *(Ephesians 3:16-17)*

🍎 **Paula** . . .We need to recognize also that it is usually when the pastor has been prophetic in his understanding, on target with his preaching, or especially loving in his confrontation, that he is apt to receive the most persecution from his congregation. This was our experience in the pastorate. At those time when John, in his searching for truth, was somewhat off base and would preach super liberal or esoteric sermons that really didn't get at things in people's hearts, they loved and idolized him. But when he was back on track and preached the Word powerfully, and the Spirit of God was penetrating people's defenses to the deep parts of their hearts, the people would become frantic to stop it. *"Get rid of the message. Get rid of the pastor."* They would do anything rather than face the deeply suppressed issues of their hearts. That's when they would persecute—never when John was in error; always when he was right on!

Evaluating our attitudes.

We need to look at our own hearts when we find ourselves being critical of someone and ask ourselves:

♦ *"Why am I angry about that? Can it be that he (or she) is exposing an area in my life that I haven't yet dealt with?"*

We need to stand on level ground at the foot of the cross, confessing our own sin, praying:

♦ *"Lord, give me a teachable spirit and help me to see if the conflict I am experiencing is because I'm acting in fleshly piety that drives the other person to react negatively just to counter-balance me."*

♦ *"Lord, am I out-of-balance so the other person has to compensate for something in me that hasn't yet been fully submitted to You for forgiveness and cleansing?"*

♦ *"Lord, what are You wanting to show me about my own heart? Bring my sin and unforgiveness to death. Set me free to be a blessing to others."*

Death of self and rebirth in love and forgiveness through Jesus Christ is worthy to be the central focus of our life. Achieving this goal is a day-by-day, hour-by-hour, moment-by-moment exercise.

Gracious Lord,

How wonderful it is that You are revealing to the Church in this day the secrets of the Kingdom—that You have given us birth and second birth in the day in which You are teaching the Church what it is to be sanctified.

You are revealing to the Church that which we have never really known before—how to cleanse our hearts so that we may be pure before You.

Lord, we want to understand more about forgiveness and we want to walk daily, both in the confidence of being forgiven our sins, and as gracious forgivers of those who sin against us.

Help us to achieve a loving and forgiving balance and counterbalance with those who share our lives. We pray that Your Holy Spirit will be our constant teacher. We thank You, Lord.

Amen

Life Application:

Balance through Forgiveness
Unity in Primary Relationships

1. What is meant by the term "being subject to Christ" (See page 117)? Write out your own definition below.

2. How is being subject to Christ different from being subject to other people?

3. Counterbalancing another person in a relationship is often good and healthy because it helps to compensate for our weaknesses. When does counterbalancing become uncomfortable (See page 118)? Discuss this with a friend or with your group members.

4. Review the section in this chapter about renouncing the demands of love (See pages 131-134).

♦ How can our love for others make demands and become manipulative? Write an example of how your love makes demands—expressed in terms of a relationship you have with someone.

♦ What does it mean to renounce the demands of love? Paraphrase that concept in your own words.

♦ Construct a statement renouncing the demands you are making in one of your relationships with another person. Then write a prayer inviting Jesus to put to death your demands and raise up in you a new way of relating.

Chapter Seven

Beyond Understanding
Grace to Cope With Life's Tragedies

෨

Even the sun seems dim
When filtered through dark branches
Of a briarpatch hidden sky.
And dreams snag against sharp thistles
Before they even begin
To rise and fly.

Yet for the faithful it is true
That fragile seeds of hope
Will still take root,
Sending forth their valiant sprigs,
Pushing ever upward
Toward the filtered rays of light.
They drink what nurture they can find
Even if only from precious drops of dew.

Lying nearly prone against the soil
It helps to know that once God's Prince
Was challenged with a crown of thorns.
He rose above it!
And by God's grace
So will I —
And so will you!

Lee Bowman

Stephen, a man richly blessed by God and full of spiritual power, boldly preached the message of Jesus Christ and performed many miracles and wonders among the people. But he met strong resistance from some men in the local synagogue who felt threatened by what he taught. When they could not refute what Stephen said with their own arguments, they seized him and brought him before the ruling Council where they bribed witnesses to testify falsely against him.

In defense of his teaching before the Council, Stephen spoke powerfully of the way in which God had revealed Himself through history and how the people had continually rejected the word of God. He spoke of Jesus as the anointed one of God—fulfilling their own prophecy, yet also being rejected, just as so many of God's prophets had been rejected before.

> *"How stubborn you are," Stephen went on to say. "How heathen your hearts, how deaf you are to God's message! You are just like your ancestors: you too have always resisted the Holy Spirit."*   *(Acts 7:51 TEV)*

> *As the members of the council listened to Stephen, they became furious and ground their teeth at him in anger. But Stephen, full of the Holy Spirit, looked up to heaven and saw God's glory and Jesus standing on the right side of God. "Look," he said. "I see heaven opened and the Son of Man standing at the right side of God."*   *(Acts 7:54-56 TEV)*

> *With a loud cry the Council members covered their ears with their hands. Then they all rushed him at once, threw him out of the city, and stoned him. The witnesses left their cloaks in the care of a young man named Saul.*
>
> *They kept on stoning Stephen as he called out to the Lord, "Lord Jesus, receive my spirit!" He knelt down and cried out in a loud voice, "Lord! Do not remember this sin against them!" He said this and died.*   *(Acts 7:54-60 TEV)*

What a tragedy of injustice! Stephen spoke only of the truth he had found in Jesus Christ, yet he became a victim of others' fear, hate, and religious intolerance. There was no repentance in the hearts of those in the religious establishment, and the murderers were never held accountable in this world for their crime.

But there was a surprising degree of forgiveness and mercy in the heart of Stephen. His life had been so changed by the love of Christ that he was able to plead forgiveness for his attackers even while they were in the act of stoning him to death. There is perhaps no better example of how the Holy Spirit can perform miracles of love in those who are willing to choose forgiveness and leave vengeance to the Lord.

By the standards of our world, extending forgiveness is a radical position for a person to take in the face of extreme hurt, cruelty, or injustice. The very idea seems to violate our sense of right and wrong. It runs contrary to natural responses to hurt and betrayal. When we suffer abuse or feel overwhelmed with injustices in life, it seems natural to want to lash out to even the score, or to punish those who have injured us.

In the terribly trying years following the death of Stephen, many Christians in the early church were put to the test. They were not criminals and didn't deserve to die, yet they were martyred for their beliefs. Christians became innocent victims of hate, religious prejudice, political expediency, and gross barbarism by a culture which seemingly had lost all reverence for human life. They were stoned to death, crucified, beheaded, impaled, and fed to wild animals as sport in the arenas. The Roman government sought to destroy the early church, but through it all, the church flourished and grew.

Many historians have said the impact of the early church on the culture of the Roman world had less to do with the way Christians lived and more to do with the way they faced death. With Stephen and other early martyrs as an example, they steadfastly refused to renounce their Lord under threat of death, chose to forgive their persecutors in Jesus' name, and went to their deaths with an incredible demonstration of courage. The Holy Spirit equipped early Christians with a spiritual strength that became such an example to others that eventually the body of Christ won over the very government that had for so long persecuted it.

Today, as in New Testament times, many people experience situations in life which call for extraordinary inner strength with which to simply cope with their sufferings. Physical brutality and emotional woundings are everywhere around us. Daily newspapers are virtual catalogs listing episodes of thefts, muggings, kidnappings, abuses, rapes, murders, and a broad variety of politically or racially motivated persecutions. Many of these crimes are clearly committed against people who are victims in the true sense of the word. They neither invite nor cause their injury. Often intense responses to being wronged come out of the victim's anger, frustration, and injustice.

When criminals are brought to trial, the most common response of those who have been wronged is to demand the full measure of retribution allowed by law. This sense of justice appeals to the Old Testament formula of "an eye for an eye and a tooth for a tooth." Unfortunately, responses to crimes or to injustices often are generalized beyond the perpetrators to direct condemnation toward the perpetrator's family, toward the culture that has provided the context for the injustice, and even toward the race or nationality of the ones involved. Vengeance becomes a pervading attitude that reaches far beyond the scope of crime or injustice and ultimately can lead to feuding, class conflict, racial and ethnic prejudice, and even the support of racial and ethnic cleansing. Both the perpetrator and everyone possibly related are vilified.

Brutality and killing, such as that spawned by inter-tribal wars in Africa, religiously motivated terrorism in the mideast, and the hate-mongering which led to the Jewish holocaust in Europe during the Second World War have not taught us the senselessness of prejudice, hate, and vengeful violence. We live in a world in which injustice and inhumanity are virtually inescapable. Both as individuals and as entire cultures, we seem more prone to respond to woundings with an attempt to get revenge rather than to seek forgiveness and reconciliation.

Many people—out of their personal frustration and hurt from being wronged—would prefer the concept of "penal" rather than "correctional" institutions for persons convicted of crimes. Criminals often are perceived as unforgivable monsters who either should be put to death or put in prison permanently. It is common for family members of victims to be quoted as "angry and incensed" that the convicted felon would someday have a chance to be paroled, or "devastated" that the convicted murderer was not given the death penalty.

Captive to our own pain and anger.

Consider what it does to us if we reduce those who wrong us to the role of unforgivable monsters. Viewing someone as a monster gives that person the power to condemn us to live with the hurting memory of our painful past. We give them the power to keep on hurting us and to stay in control of our lives. Is that what we want?

This is not to say that forgiveness should mean looking the other way as if hurts and injustices had not happened. We cannot deny evil or even try to tolerate it without confrontation. As Lewis Smedes says in his book, *Forgive and Forget:* "There is no real forgiveness unless there is first relentless exposure and honest judgment. When we forgive evil, we do not excuse it, we do not tolerate it. We look evil full in the face, call it what it is, let its horror shock and stun and enrage us, and only then do we forgive it."[1]

From time to time we catch a glimpse of praise-worthy exceptions to ingrained bitterness when Christians have called on the deepest resources of God's grace to accomplish forgiveness in the midst of intense pain and suffering.

Peter and Ann Pretorius are South African missionaries, working in association with American evangelist James Robison to bring food and medical relief to needy people in southern Africa. The Christian commitment of this couple enabled them to move from a traditional stance of apartheid in their homeland to view people of all races as God's children, equally deserving of our love and justice. While doing relief work among black populations, their faith was severely tested when Ann's sister and brother-in-law were brutally bludgeoned to death by the notorious "hammer man" serial killer who targeted white families for robbery and murder.

In a televised testimony, Ann recounts how she experienced a great anointing of God's grace which allowed her to say of this black man who murdered her sister, *"Forgive him, Lord, for he knew not what he was doing."* Because of their choosing forgiveness, Ann and her husband have been able to continue a loving and compassionate ministry among blacks where otherwise they might have succumbed to bitterness and hate.

Another striking example came to light on the Leeza Gibbons television show in which she interviewed the parents of Jeffrey Dahmer, convicted of horrendous rapes, murders and cannibalizing of numerous young boys in Chicago. When asked whether they had been judged and badly treated by others for the crimes their son committed, they replied that they had in many ways. However, the notable exception was the acceptance and friendship they have received from several parents of their son's victims. Motivated by deep Christian faith, these parents have reached past their grief in a spirit of compassion and forgiveness that overcame the horror of those terrible crimes.

Fortunately, not all of us will have to suffer the trauma of being victims of crimes as terrible as these, or of having to bear up under the stress of such crimes committed against those we love or by those we love. However, most of us will have to deal with other circumstances which will try our souls and our faith. Tragic accidents, illnesses, divorce, betrayals, and financial setbacks are so common that virtually every one of us will be confronted with several major crises of faith in our life. Love of God does not isolate us from trials and suffering.

As stated in chapter four, we need to be honest by confessing to God our anger against Him and against others whom we perceive have wronged us. God is not guilty of anything and certainly does not need our forgiveness. Our anger and unforgiveness are our own and grow out of our need to be in control. However, God can use every circumstance of life to bring blessing to us and to write wisdom in our hearts if we respond according to His will.

> *And we know that God causes all things to work together for good to those who love God, to those who are called according to His purpose.*   *(Romans 8:28 NAS)*

When we are abused, when we are victims of crime, when circumstances weigh upon us, or when we are out of control because of the general injustices of life, we are not without hope. God promises victory as we act on our faith and sow forgiveness, pray blessing into our circumstances, and trust in God's mercy to heal our wounds and provide for our every need.

Consider the following examples of those who reaped the grace of God by sowing forgiveness that goes beyond understanding.

Facing financial crisis and loss of life's work.

After fifteen years of hard work planning and developing the nation's largest general aviation airport and industrial park in suburban St. Louis, Paul and Gretel Haglin had just gotten the project to the point of standing on its own and were on the threshold of realizing their dream of becoming multi-millionaires.

At this otherwise positive milestone in the Haglins' business career, the insurance company that put together their multi-million dollar financial loan package was cited by the Securities and Exchange Commission for fraud related to a totally unrelated business deal. As a result of the citation for fraud, the Texas Insurance Board forced the insurance company to call in all their real estate loans, including the Haglins'.

Paul and Gretel were absolutely stunned because in the time they were allotted to pay off the recalled loan, it was impossible to find alternate refinancing. Consequently, the insurance company that held their loan, after previously having been cited for fraud, declared the Haglins' loan in default and literally stole the entire project through foreclosure.

This turn of events seemed almost too much to bear for the Haglins. The loan was in good shape and was adequately protected, but the forced recall caused them to lose everything. The recall had nothing to do with their airport project and they had done nothing wrong. It was simply because the lenders in some totally unrelated business transaction had been wickedly dishonest.

The Haglins' response to this incredible financial blow is a real testimony to how God's grace accomplishes miracles for those who choose to take the high road to forgiveness. The following account is in Paul's own words.

Paul Haglin

We thought, "How could this happen to us?" We had tried hard to be good stewards of what God had given us. God had blessed us and graced us by putting this project together, and we had tried to be righteous in our business dealings as we went along. There certainly had been a lot of tests. We were tempted by others to pay bribe money and to pay people to withhold information. But each time we were faced with a short-cut decision, we heard the Spirit of God say "No! That's not the way I want you to walk!" In every case we obeyed God and chose the ethical high road. Then this setback happened to us, and we lost everything.

We knew that if we did not choose immediately to forgive, to release, and to pray blessings on those who were so spitefully using us, we were going to be in deep trouble with resentment, demands for revenge, and all manner of ungodly things that would come to eat us up.

I think Gretel and I did pretty well considering the immensity of the problem. But our faithful secretary, Susie, had a very hard time with it. I think it is sometimes more difficult to have something horrendous happen to a loved one than it is to experience it ourselves. We don't always have the amount of grace to apply on their behalf that God gives us when we are stressed ourselves.

We recognized this with our secretary, so I started praying with her three times a day—when we came into the office in the morning, when we broke for lunch, and before we left for home at night. We prayed together, and we started to pray blessings on those insurance people who were taking everything from us that we had worked so hard to achieve.

We prayed about not getting bitter and we prayed about forgiveness. We took layer after layer off the onion of our hurt. Each layer brought fresh tears. Gretel and I were fighting bitterness, and we were helping Susie fight as well. We were fighting together so we would not let our feelings turn to hate.

As we continued to pray day after day, our feelings changed. We began to feel that we really did want God to bless these people. Our testimony is that finally, on the day when that prayer-soaked vice president from the insurance company came with his two lawyers to take our company, there was literally nothing in our hearts but love for those men.

My secretary got up and treated them as though they were the finest customers we ever had. *"May I take your coat, sir? Would you like a cup of coffee, sir?"* Nothing but love came from her.

As we sat there in the conference room across the table from each other, we were surrounded by God's grace and He was literally in our presence, guarding us. Susie sat in an anteroom where she could look in on our discussions. She had a vision as I was sitting there talking about these papers, signing our life away; she could see Jesus standing behind me, reading over my shoulder and guiding me in what to say. I called their attention to one section of the papers that seemed to take matters too far. They immediately agreed and had the section corrected and retyped.

When they walked out with everything we owned, there was peace. We were able to conduct that transfer without agony and without disappointing bitterness because we had done what God had asked us to do.

The amazing end to this story is that on the way to the airport, the vice president had his driver stop. He got out of the car and went to a pay phone to call me. Susie and I were still in the office cleaning up after everything had been taken. On the phone he stammered around a bit and finally said, *"Paul, I just had to call you to say thank you. You made my job so easy for me."*

Of course, then I had another problem. I had to deal with God for asking me to make his job easy for him. But that was nothing compared to what we'd been through.

Then the vice president said, *"I felt such a peace in your office."* This insurance company officer felt the peace of God that surpasses human understanding even while he was totally ripping us off. That is an awesome testimony.

We have often found comfort in recalling the story of Joseph from the Old Testament. His jealous brothers had sold him into slavery and reported to his father that he was dead. Joseph had every reason to be bitter, but he withheld his judgment of them out of reverence for his God.

Years later, when Joseph was in great authority in Egypt and his brothers came before him begging for food in a time of famine, he didn't seek revenge. Rather, he wept for joy that they could be reunited and he blessed them with his protection and provision. Joseph said to his brothers:

*Do not be afraid, for am I in God's place? And as for you,
you meant evil against me, but God meant it for good in order
to bring about this present result, to preserve many people
alive.   (Genesis 50:19-20 NAS)*

The lesson here is not just about Joseph, a story in the Bible.
There is a spiritual principle that will work with each of us. No
matter what happens to us, we do not have to be debilitated by disappointment or be consumed with thoughts of anger or revenge.
We don't have to. If we choose the high road, God will be with us.

* Paul and Gretel Haglin, Resurrection Christian Ministries
   Eagles Nest Farm, Route 1, Box 62A, Hawk Point, MO 63349

Coping with life-long pain and physical disability.

Judy Beemiller will always be remembered by friends and family for her indomitable spirit, positive attitude, kindness toward everyone she met, and her enduring Christian faith. Reflecting on her own life, Judy wrote a poem that reveals the special kind of focus she had developed. In one stanza she proclaimed the following:

I'll work and I'll strive for my future—
For the treasures this world can't provide,
For my treasures, they're stored up in heaven
Up there, by the Master's side.

This poem is especially poignant because Judy had a lot she could have been resentful about regarding the "treasures" life had brought her. Judy was a double amputee with numerous other health problems including heart trouble and diabetes.

As a very young child she developed dermatomyositis, a rare disease that causes the calcification of the muscles. The illness caused extreme pain throughout her life, forced amputation of both her legs, and caused her to lose the use of one arm and partial use of the other. Yet Judy never considered herself to be disabled. She preferred the term "physically challenged." Her health problems presented her with a life-long struggle that she never let give in to bitterness. Rather, she approached her physical challenges as obstacles that needed to be overcome, and she joyfully celebrated each small victory.

When her illness was diagnosed at the age of eight, the doctors gave her only a few years to live and told her parents to make her as comfortable as possible in the time she had left. Instead, she lived at home for the next eleven years. At the age of nineteen, shortly after moving into the residential facility at Los Angeles County's Rancho Los Amigos Medical Center, Judy had both legs amputated. Unable to use the prescribed prostheses because of the intense pain, she was fitted with an electric wheel chair and subsequently experienced her first glimpse of independence.

She spent the next twelve years as a resident at Rancho Los Amigos whirling throughout that vast medical complex in her wheelchair. She took classes, got her high school diploma, volunteered to work with newly disabled patients, and befriended everyone with her indomitable spirit, infectious grin, and caring attitude. Despite her own problems, she became an inspiration to others, blessing all who knew her.

When Rancho Los Amigos became strictly a rehabilitation facility, Judy and a friend moved to a two bedroom apartment across the street. She developed even more skills in independent living and was able to go shopping, take the bus to church, and continue her education—obtaining an associate degree in special education from Ceritos College. She continued to work with children in the Rancho classrooms, became very active in lobbying for legislative issues supporting the disabled, and even sang in her church choir. In 1987 she was selected from among some 79,000 volunteers to be named one of the six "Distinguished Volunteers of the Year" for Los Angeles County.

Despite her limitations, Judy Beemiller believed that she led a charmed life. Once, when being interviewed by a reporter for a feature story, Judy stopped to ask, *"This isn't going to be one of those sob stories, is it? One time a friend of mine was interviewed by a newspaper, and when we read the article we all cried. We didn't realize we were so bad off."*

Judy died at the age of 51 as the result of a tragic accident when her van inadvertently backed into her wheelchair and overturned it. Injuries to her frail body brought on complications that resulted in heart failure. But her legacy lives on. Her positive response to the hard knocks in life never allowed bitterness to settle in her heart. Her kindness, positive attitude, and empathy with others kept her open to all life had to offer and allowed her to focus on how God would empower her to overcome. In testimony to her faith, she penned the following poem not long before her death:

My cross in this world is heavy,
And I'll carry it my whole life through
For you see I will never be able
To walk in this world as you do.

People ask how I can have faith
And love God who permits this to be,
And I answer as honest and open
As a heart full of His love can be.

If it weren't for my Heavenly Father
Who sent His Son down here for me,
If it weren't for my dear blessed Savior
Who in love died on Calvary's tree,

There'd be no dreams or hopes for my future
I'd be lost 'neath the wages of sin.
But I can keep right on smiling
For He's put His love down deep within.

So I'll work and I'll strive for the future
For the treasures this world can't provide,
For my treasures, they're stored up in heaven
Up there, by my Master's side.

One day when my work here is ended
And I'm called to my home on high,
With a heart full of love I will thank Him
That He chose for my sins to die.

So you see why my heart is so glad.
One day I'll be gloriously clad.
I'll walk and I'll run around heaven,
I'll sing and I'll shout with joy!

And from there I shall live forever
In God's peace and His tranquillity.
For you see the words of the Master
Have especially come true for me.

Judy Beemiller

Dear Lord,

I understand that just by being a Christian we cannot expect to escape the hard knocks in life, or even the cruel injustices that may come our way. But everywhere I look, I see pain and suffering, touching even my friends and family. I want to stand tall in faith and be a strong example of one who affirms life, but it is difficult. I often feel weak and I'm tempted to despair.

Lord, I ask that You take this burden from me. Lift me when my spirit falls. Equip me through Your Holy Spirit to be so grounded in Your love that I can walk with a sense of peace and confidence through the darkest of valleys.

Help me to know and to daily live with the assurance that You are able to work through any circumstance in life to bring good to me and to further the work of Your Kingdom.

Amen

---

1. Smedes, Lewis, *Forgive and Forget, Healing the Hurts We Don't Deserve,* San Francisco, Harper & Row, 1984, p. 79.

Life Application:
Beyond Understanding
Grace to Cope With Life's Tragedies

We can never be fully prepared for tragedies that may happen. However, if we are well grounded in our trust of a righteous and loving God, and have sorted through those values that are important in life, we can be better prepared to cope when the unexpected happens—and hopefully to choose forgiveness.

With a friend or your group members, discuss how you think you might respond if the following situations were to happen to you. Do you think your response would be typical of the general population, or would you choose to respond in a different manner?

Where is God in these situations? How do you balance holding a person accountable for their actions and your ability to be forgiving?

A family tragedy.
You go shopping with your family to a nearby mall and while you are gone, several neighborhood children playing with fireworks accidentally set your house on fire. When you return, you find your home burned to the ground, destroying everything you own except the clothes you are wearing.

Accidental death of a loved one.
Your teenage daughter goes to a party at a classmate's home with her boyfriend. While there, they do some drinking. Driving home, the young man misses a curve and runs his car into a tree. Your daughter is killed instantly. The young man escapes with minor injuries. He is remorseful and begs your forgiveness.

Robbery and violence.

Coming home from a movie one night, you are accosted in your driveway by two young men who demand money. They become angry with what you have to give them and brutally beat you, causing injuries that require three months convalescence and tens of thousands of dollars in medical bills. When they are caught and brought to trial, you learn they come from broken homes where there was a history of physical abuse and drug use.

Chapter Eight

Restoration of Christian Unity
Forgiveness at the Heart of God's Kingdom

৯৹

Our talking is a sacred ship
Which plies the deep
And brings, piece by piece,
The precious cargo of our lives
From distant shores.

Forgiveness is a bridge
That we must build
To cross our gulf of separateness,
To find where ending meets beginning,
And hard journeys reach completion.

Togetherness is to talk, to touch,
To bridge our separateness
And reach out in love
For the hand that, perhaps,
Could let us fall.
That's what makes life worth it all.
Togetherness.

                             Lee Bowman

B ridging our separateness from others is what forgiveness is all about. Such bridge-building requires piecing together new relationships through presence, communication, mutual understanding, and acceptance. It is an awesome task, but incredibly worthwhile and rewarding. What is it then that we need to understand about forgiveness? Let's review!

♦ Forgiveness is a necessity—to be forgiven by God, we must be forgiving toward others. We must work out our salvation by responding positively in forgiveness to God's gift of grace.

♦ Forgiveness can often be easy if we practice it as a daily discipline, but it becomes more difficult as we allow our hurts and resentments to linger and deepen into bitterness.

♦ Forgiveness is a major battle when hurts become lodged in the heart and spirit and become part of our root nature.

♦ Forgiveness is achievable through the Lord Jesus Christ if we so surrender our thinking and behaving to Him that every circumstance of life may be used for His good purposes.

Until now, we have been looking at the issue of forgiveness from the perspective of our own salvation and sanctification. But now let's try to see forgiveness from God's point of view.

Why did God pay the price of sacrificing his Son to return us to right relationship with Him? Why didn't He just wipe us out and start all over? Did He provide for forgiveness and our salvation just because He loved us so much as individuals?

Perhaps love for us as individuals would have been enough. But God sees His creation from a much broader perspective. God wants to restore us because He wants to build unity. He wants to build a kingdom of sons and daughters.

The first sin fractured unity. It broke the unity between mankind and heaven. It fractured the unity between man and woman. It destroyed the unity between man and nature.

> *Cursed is the ground because of you; through painful toil you will eat of it all the days of your life. It will produce thorns and thistles for you, and you will eat the plants of the field. By the sweat of your brow you will eat your food until you return to the ground, since from it you were taken; for dust you are and to dust you will return.* (Genesis 3:17-18)

God is interested in more than just our personal salvation. He wants us to share in the restoration of unity throughout creation, fulfilling His purpose throughout the heavens. Through the Church, He wants to bring all creation into His eternal purpose:

> *The creation waits in eager expectation for the sons of God to be revealed. For the creation was subjected to frustration not by its own choice, but by the will of the one who subjected it, in hope that the creation itself will be liberated from its bondage to decay and brought into the glorious freedom of the children of God.* (Romans 8:19-21)

> *His intent was that now, through the church, the manifold wisdom of God should be made known to the rulers and authorities in the heavenly realms, according to his eternal purpose which he accomplished in Christ Jesus our Lord.* (Ephesians 3:10-11)

> *. . . make my joy complete by being in the same mind, maintaining the same love, united in spirit, intent on one purpose.* (Philippians 2:12)

The message for us is that forgiveness is the very ground of unity for the restoration of the Kingdom of God.

> *How good and pleasant it is when brothers live together in unity! It is like precious oil poured on the head, running down*

*on the beard, running down on Aaron's beard, down upon the
collar of his robes. It is as if the dew of Hermon were falling
on Mount Zion. For there the Lord bestows his blessing, even
life forevermore.*   *(Psalm 133:1,3)*

When a priest was ordained in the time of King David, the high
priest anointed him with oil. Not just a dab of oil—they poured it
on until it rolled down over his head and neck, spilling onto his
robes. The anointing was the high point of celebration because,
through the priest, all the people of his region would come into
their destiny.

The ordination was a great celebration of unity. In this Psalm
of David, he tells us that to live in unity is to be refreshed and to be
showered with God's blessing of life, forevermore.

After years of traveling around speaking in one church after
another, we can sense immediately whether there is unity or disunity within a church body. If there is disunity, there will be heaviness, rancor, and distrust. If there is unity, there is lightness, joy,
and a sense of blessing pouring over all. Forgiveness restores unity,
and only where unity exists can blessing be poured out.

This is true for marriages as well. When married couples fall
out of loving relationship with each other and go through divorce in
a spirit of unforgiveness, the results are spread far beyond their personal relationship. Their children suffer. Even their adult children
suffer. The blessings lost in the breaking of their unity subsequently
are lost to friends and other relatives as well. Bitterness spreads and
can damage even the innocent far removed.

We have noted that often tragic circumstances fall upon the
children of parents who have split up in bitter unforgiveness. Almost always when we see a tragic death of a teenager, we find that
some kind of drastic fragmentation has happened previously between the parents. Their disunity fractured the cover of protection
and blessing over their children.

We don't want to make this into an unalterable judgment so as
to say to all those who have lost a child or a close relative that they
are at fault because they were out of unity. That is not always the
case. Many other factors may have opened the door to trouble. But
we must recognize that we are created to live in corporateness. We

can never successfully be islands unto ourselves. We share in bless-ing as we live in unity because we are vital links in many kinds of family relationships. Likewise, we share in pain when fractured unity blocks the fullness of blessing.

Consider the prayer of Jesus:

I will remain in the world no longer, but they are still in the world, and I am coming to you. Holy Father, protect them by the power of Your name—the name You gave Me—so that they may be one as We are one . . .

My prayer is not for them alone. I pray also for those who will believe in Me through their message, that all of them may be one, Father, just as You are in Me and I am in You. May they also be in Us so the world may believe that You have sent Me. I have given them the glory that You have given Me, that they may be one as We are one: I in them and You in Me. May they be brought to complete unity to let the world know that You sent Me and have loved them even as You have loved Me. *(John 17:11, 20-23)*

In this passage we can't help but feel the intense yearning of the Lord's heart for us to come into the unity He wants for us. What grieving He must feel because of our lack of unity! He has given us many gifts so that we might become one with each other and with Him. Yet so often the Church has not used those gifts for unity, but to promote disunity. It seems to be a law that however wonderful a gift from God, to that degree we can and will misuse it to disunity and harm!

The Lord gave us water baptism as an expression of repen-tance for our sins—to be buried with Him in water and resurrected to new life. That was designed to bring us into unity with Him and with one another. And yet we manage to argue with one another about how and when water baptism should be applied, how much water is needed, and who's doing it right and who isn't.

The Lord gave us communion that we might experience deep fellowship with one another and with Him. And yet we argue about what it means, how it should be served, and about who's doing it in a valid way and who isn't.

He gave us the baptism of the Holy Spirit that we might be united in His Spirit. Yet what division and rancor has often arisen in the Church over the gifts of the Holy Spirit and how various gifts should find expression in the lives of those who use them!

He gave us understanding about inner healing and transformation of the inner man so we might be enabled to deal with the deep things of the heart and come into unity with God and others. Yet, what disunity has resulted because we have not really tuned ourselves to God's heart! We argue about whether inner healing is biblical and whether and how we should be involved in it. We have not focused on Him and poured our energy into what He is doing in the healing and transforming process.

We have had many eruptions of disunity over contrasting theories of what holiness is. Holiness is a state of having been cleansed by the Lord, identifying with Him, and participating in His purity of mind and heart and spirit. But we would seek to categorize holiness—each in his own possessive and divisive way. We attach limiting names and definitions to holiness, judge one another according to our own idea of who is holy and who is not, and measure who is more elevated in holiness than someone else. In doing so, we greatly defile the gifts of God.

The discipline of forgiveness in the Body of Christ.

We believe there is a distinctive discipline one must maintain regularly over one's own heart to be pure before the Lord—a discipline of forgiveness. Lack of this discipline throughout the Body of Christ is an issue we have grieved about for years. Why does the Body of Christ fail to catch the vision of forgiveness? Why does the Body of Christ remain so lazy about keeping the heart clean and clear? Why does the Body of Christ avoid the practical daily discipline of forgiving others?

We do not come into good and true repentance because we have little awareness of the Kingdom of God. We don't understand how our unforgiveness shatters the Kingdom of God. We so lack love for the Kingdom that it matters little to us anyway.

All too often we hear some brother saying *"Well, I only hurt myself. I don't hurt anybody else, I guess I'm my own worst enemy!"*

That's a total lack of awareness of the Kingdom. We need to ask, *"Are we preaching the same message Jesus preached?"* Our focus seems to be on individual sin, forgiveness, and salvation. But wherever Jesus went, He preached the Kingdom of God—how being restored to right relationship with God should restore us to right relationship with our fellow man within the Kingdom.

Jesus wants to build such corporateness that we realize fully we are not just separate individuals, we are in a marriage and a family. We are so united to one another that everything that happens to my brother or sister is critical to what happens to me! Their life is my very life. That is the Kingdom of God.

There is that in us that actually makes a fetish of enjoying pain. We feel more worthwhile if we are suffering, and we too often believe we suffer alone. We talk to people like we *"just have to bear that cross."* We like being noble martyrs and have little awareness of how our sin and pain effects others and drags them down as well. We don't understand that our brother needs *us* to be whole in order for *him* to be whole. Our pain destroys his celebration.

In love with the Kingdom of God.

We need to be in love with what Jesus is in love with—the whole Kingdom of God. We don't love what He loves enough to pay the price of linkage to our brothers and sisters and to take personal responsibility for unity within the Kingdom. We personalize and trivialize our own particular sin and pain because we have not caught the vision of corporateness.

When we have a limited view of our role in the Kingdom, we don't repent of how we contribute to fracturing unity. We tend to connect repentance only with our own individual salvation.

Good repentance is when the Lord's love for his total family so fills us that we repent of the way our sin and unforgiveness rapes the Body of Christ of the unity the Lord so loves. A good repentance is not just that we get straightened out, but that we repent for the sake of the Church and the entire family of God.

What happens when we hang on to unforgiveness?

1. If we harbor unforgiveness, there is no way we can see reality—all we have is our own subjective perceptions.

The eye is the lamp of the body. If your eyes are good, your whole body will be full of light. But if your eyes are bad, your whole body will be full of darkness. If then the light within you is darkness, how great is that darkness!   (Matthew 6:22-23)

The responses we make to the circumstances and events of our life when we are very young determine the way we are apt to respond to events throughout life. Unforgiveness learned early in life is like mud in our eyes. It keeps us from seeing with clarity and truth because we are so bothered by what has happened to us previously.

A typical example of this was when a young woman came to us for counseling, complaining that her father had always yelled at her. She described how she would fall into terrible fear whenever her father would raise his voice. Any present confrontation with him made her want to flee. Consequently their relationship had broken down, and there was virtually no discussion or understanding between them.

The actual fact was that in their recent history her father seldom really yelled at her, but she perceived it that way because of how often he had expressed himself with anger when she was a child. At that time, he was immature, didn't yet know the Lord, and had not come to repentance. Those frightful experiences of being yelled at as a child were burned into her heart. She had never forgiven him and was not able to let go of that original hurtful response. Even a quiet reprimand from him was now perceived as angry shouting. Her failure to let go of unforgiveness was blocking her from having a loving relationship with her father—and with others.

This young woman's unforgiveness spilled over into other relationships as well. Whenever anyone from the Body of Christ

would come to her to speak the truth in love, she would perceive it
as critical yelling at her. Thus, her unforgiveness of her father fractured her relationships with others. She was seriously concerned
that she responded this way to her father and to others, but she
didn't know how to overcome her inward spontaneous reactions of
anger, fear, and flight.

In his letter to the Roman church, St. Paul revealed the struggle he had between his mind, committed to the law of God, and his
sin nature, held captive to the law of sin.

> *So I find this law at work: when I want to do good, evil is right*
> *there with me. For in my inner being I delight in God's law,*
> *but I see another law at work in the members of my body,*
> *waging war against the law of my mind and making me a pris-*
> *oner to the law of sin at work within my members. What a*
> *wretched man I am! Who will rescue me from this body of*
> *death? Thanks be to God—through Jesus Christ our Lord!*
> *(Romans 7:21-25)*

Paul is speaking here of more than just the physical body. He is
speaking of the entire "body" of the way people think and feel, the
sin nature lodged in our hearts against which our renewed minds
must do battle. That "body" of the way we think and feel is not
ours alone, it is part of the corporate structure in which all of us
live.

There are unregenerate elements in the culture that surround
us—the way our family thinks and feels, the way our friends think
and feel, even the way our church thinks and feels. If we don't
crucify the negative and sinful ways of thinking, feeling, and acting,
they will impair and destroy the unity in which God intends to bless
our family, friends, and church. That's the corporate expression of
the law of sin. And as Paul says, *"Who will rescue me from this*
body of death?"

In teaching various groups as we travel, we frequently encounter people who are immensely insecure in who they are because
they have not received enough wholesome nurture, but they have
received much criticism throughout their lives. The insecurity be-

comes evident when individuals begin to take personally what is said in a general group discussion of common problems. Rather than hearing the discussion for what it is and applying whatever principles fit, they feel offended or accused, as if the discussion were focusing solely on them.

When this happens, we have often found ourselves trapped in a no-win situation. If someone is threatened by what is being said and we look at them during the discussion, they become sure they are being targeted for criticism. On the other hand, if we don't look at them, they're sure we're rejecting them. This happens simply because, due to unforgiveness, they are unable to see reality as it is.

2. When we hang on to unforgiveness, our discernment becomes warped because we interpret issues from a childish point of view.

The unforgiving ways we hold within us are actually childish ways. When we are unforgiving, we see, feel, and respond childishly. The way of forgiveness and love causes increasing maturity that provides real answers and real resolutions for problems. The Apostle Paul reminded the Corinthian church of this:

When I was a child I used to speak as a child, think as a child, reason as a child; but when I became a man, I did away with childish things. For now we see in a mirror dimly, but then face to face; now I know in part, but then I shall know fully just as I also have been fully known.

(1 Corinthians 13:11-12 NAS)

He also reminded them of the opposite, which happens when the disciplined way of forgiveness has not become ours.

I gave you milk, not solid food, for you were not yet ready for it. Indeed, you are still not ready. For since there is jealousy and quarreling among you, are you not worldly?

(1 Corinthians 3:2-3)

When the Lord has dealt with the mud in our eyes and with the confusion in our spirits, we'll see with clarity and discernment. Here is an illustration of how one's discernment becomes warped.

A husband may feel genuine affection for his wife and decide to bring home a gift because he wants to bless her heart. But if previous hurts, especially in childhood, have lodged unforgiveness in her heart toward people she thinks have tried to manipulate her by gifts, or toward people who gave her gifts of things rather than the loving gift of themselves, then she has false eyes and doesn't have true discernment to see what is actually in her husband's heart. She is apt to assign wrong motives to his gifts. She may feel that he is only trying to manipulate her because he wants something.

In another case, a wife may have a natural propensity to show affection toward her husband by hugging, snuggling, or kissing him frequently. But if he grew up with negative feelings and unforgiveness toward others who used such behavior to smother or control him, then he may not have the discernment to read his wife's affection as real and pure. He may feel smothered or abused. He will then activate childish ways, like looking in a carnival mirror and seeing a distorted reflection of reality. He won't be able to receive his wife's sincere feelings and he won't see himself rightly.

What should one's repentance be in cases such as this? How should we repent? If we often fail to recognize our spouse's approaches as love, our repentance should not merely be that we failed to receive love, but that we fractured the unity of our family. That is the repentance which is appropriate to the Lord. We should pray:

Lord, I have fractured the unity of my family. I have failed to allow myself to be blessed. That has wounded my partner and fractured our unity. Forgive me Lord, that I have broken the unity of our family.

As Christians, we lose our message to the world if we do not live in the unity we profess. We must recognize how important unity is and protect it with appropriate repentances and forgiveness.

*Be completely humble and gentle; be patient, bearing with one
another in love. Make every effort to keep the unity of the
Spirit through the bond of peace.*   *(Ephesians 4:2-3)*

Unity doesn't mean uniformity. Unity doesn't mean we are
never to fight. We need to talk things out, even if that means hassles with one another. That is not yet disunity. Disunity results
when fights are accompanied by withdrawing of the heart. But if
our quarreling is undergirded with repentance, respect for one another, and forgiveness, the unity of our relationship stays intact.

**3. Choosing to be unforgiving causes us to fall short of the
grace of God.**

*See to it that no one comes short of the grace of God; that no
root of bitterness springing up causes trouble, and by it many
be defiled.*   *(Hebrews 12:15 NAS)*

When and how does a Christian miss or come short of the
grace of God? Suppose there is a man named Bob, working in an
office. One afternoon his boss jumps all over him, saying: *"Bob, you
have really screwed up everything you've tried to do today. What
is the matter with you?"*

That criticism really hurts, and Bob goes into a depressive
mood because it hooks into the way his father used to berate him.
But while Bob is inwardly wrestling with that, his co-worker Jim
steps up and says to the boss in Bob's presence, *"Wait a minute,
you're off base here. What happened today was not Bob's fault. He
did his job just as he was asked to do, and if it went wrong it was
because of other factors."*

Then another co-worker speaks up and says, *"That's right, I
can vouch for the fact that Bob did all that he was supposed to do.
He doesn't deserve any blame."*

Later on, while Bob is talking with his friends, he says, *"You
know, when I get into trouble, nobody ever defends me!"*

Bob never heard what his friends did for him. It was God's
grace to cause them to speak up and defend him. That support was

part of the blessed corporateness God brought into his life, but he didn't recognize or acknowledge it. He fell short of God's grace.

Bob's response wounded his brothers because it was evident he never saw what they had done for him. Subsequently, they thought, *"Why did we ever open our mouths to defend him? He never even acknowledged we were doing it."* Because of unforgiveness, the unity of the workplace was further fractured when it could have been salvaged.

Or, look at an office situation in another way. The boss comes in the office and gives Bob an affirmation. He says, *"Bob, you really did a good job today."* But then he adds a comment about how one issue could have been handled better.

Bob failed to receive the compliment. He retained only that one word of criticism. Then his friends came to him and said, *"Hey, didn't you hear how pleased he was with your work?"*

And Bob says, *"No, I didn't. He's always finding fault with me."*

That is what fractures unity. Bob couldn't hear the reality of compliments because his mind was clouded with lingering unforgivenesses toward his unduly critical father. For Bob, his repentance needs to include more than his inability to hear or for his blindness in misunderstanding, but for the role he played in fracturing unity in the office.

Bob should pray repentantly, *"Lord, forgive me. You wanted to build unity and love relationships among my co-workers, and I fractured that."*

❧ *John* . . . In my own case, my mother used to work me long hours. I had two cows to milk, 300 chickens to feed, a 38-tree orchard and an acre and a half of garden to take care of. I worked from morning till night, but it seemed I didn't get compliments from my mother. I didn't get the affirmation I needed, and my heart became bitter about that.

It isn't important now whether my mother did or didn't compliment my hard work as a boy. What is important is that I judged her for how she treated me, and my judgments eventually resulted in my own inability to give compliments to my children.

*You, therefore, have no excuse, you who have passed judgment
on someone else, for at whatever point you judge the other,
you are condemning yourself, because you who pass judgment
do the same things.* *(Romans 2:1)*

Realizing this, I had to come into repentance. But my repentance needed to be for more than my judgments on my mother, more than being sorry that I, too, found it difficult to give compliments. I needed to repent of the way my attitude and actions wounded my children and fractured the unity of the family—for their sakes.

We don't get set free unless our repentance is full and complete. When we are concerned only about our own salvation, we become sinfully self-centered. We need to catch the vision of the need for unity in the whole family and be repentant for the ways in which we have contributed to fracturing that unity.

4. When we hang on to unforgiveness, our sin comes back on us and must be dealt with again and again.

In the model prayer Jesus gave for us, he addressed God with the fairness that also should be expected from us. Jesus asked the Father to *"forgive us our trespasses as we forgive others who trespass against us."* If we are not willing to forgive others their transgressions against us, then how can we expect God to continue to forgive us our transgressions? We reap the unforgiveness we have sown and God doesn't want that.

It is true that when we come to Jesus He washes all our sins away. But if we harbor unforgiveness deep in our heart, that unforgiveness will continue to generate the same kind of sin that stained us beforehand. Like the man forgiven of ten thousand talents who would not forgive another who owed him a pittance, all our debts (sins) come back on us.

Unless we allow the Lord to deal with the root of our sinful unforgiveness, we will have to continue to struggle with the same old things again and again. Certainly we cannot expect God to continue to give us His grace if we are not willing to give the gift of grace to others.

> *Therefore, the kingdom of heaven is like a king who wanted to settle accounts with his servants. As he began the settlement, a man who owed him ten thousand talents was brought to him. Since he was not able to pay, the master ordered that he and his wife and his children and all that he had be sold to repay the debt.*
>
> *The servant fell on his knees before him. "Be patient with me," he begged, "and I will pay back everything." The servant's master took pity on him, canceled his debt and let him go.*
>
> *But when the servant went out, he found one of his fellow servants who owed him a hundred denarii. He grabbed him and began to choke him. "Pay back what you owe me," he demanded.*
>
> *His fellow servant fell to his knees and begged him, "Be patient with me, and I will pay you back."*
>
> *But he refused. Instead, he went off and had the man thrown into prison until he could pay the debt. When the other servants saw what had happened, they were greatly distressed and went and told their master everything that had happened.*
>
> *Then the master called the servant in. "You wicked servant," he said, "I canceled all that debt of yours because you begged me to. Shouldn't you have had mercy on your fellow servant just as I had on you?" In anger his master turned him over to the jailers to be tortured, until he should pay back all he owed.*
>
> *This is how the heavenly Father will treat each of you unless you forgive your brother from your heart.*
>
> *(Matthew 18:23-35)*

This is not merely a fanciful parable—it is a vivid description of the way reality actually works! We have seen it happen hundreds of times. Brothers or sisters won't forgive a perceived wrong. Soon their own bitterness turns back on them and they find themselves suffering in real mental and emotional prisons. We pay a heavy price for bitterness when we could easily receive the grace and for-giveness of the Lord.

Our unforgiveness affects unity throughout the Body when people see us holding on to wounds we should have been willing to give up.

When we seem to repent on the surface but keep falling back into ancient patterns of unforgiveness, people hurt for us. They are disappointed in us. It makes others question whether this thing called Christianity really works, since so many of those who profess to follow a forgiving Lord are so unwilling to be forgiving them-selves. Unforgiving Christians are seen as hypocritical.

And then we begin to question ourselves, asking, *"Why do I keep falling back all the time?"* We wind up in isolation. We want to hide so others won't know what is going on inside our unforgiv-ing hearts and lives. We suffer such consequences only because we don't let the Lord fully into our hearts in order to come to com-pleteness of repentance.

Many people fall into the trap of harboring bitterness and grudges while fully understanding that Christians should not behave that way. Consequently, they fall into denial and pretend that every-thing is just fine in their lives, despite the anger and bitterness within. This results in a "smiling depression" in which rage, bitter-ness, shame, guilt, and even death wishes are repressed—yet sneak out every once in a while to expose their true character.

5. Unwillingness to forgive affects our ability to confront others and to receive correction.

When we are off course morally and spiritually, we need broth-ers and sisters in Christ to take us aside, confront us lovingly, and earnestly plead with us to correct our ways. To be rebuked or to rebuke is not something to fear. We should welcome correction for our own enlightenment, and we should care enough for our friends to go to them with our legitimate concerns—caring enough about unity both to receive correction and to confront.

Stern discipline is for him who forsakes the way; He who hates reproof will die.   *(Proverbs 15:10 NAS)*

He who corrects a scoffer gets dishonor for himself, and he who reproves a wicked man gets insults for himself. Do not reprove a scoffer, lest he hate you. Reprove a wise man, and he will love you. Give instruction to a wise man and he will be still wiser. Teach a righteous man, and he will increase his learning. The fear of the Lord is the beginning of wisdom, and the knowledge of the Holy One is understanding.
(Proverbs 9:7-10 NAS)

Faithful are the wounds of a friend, but deceitful are the kisses of an enemy. *(Proverbs 27:6 NAS)*

The Bible says we are to *"speak the truth in love."* It is not love when we see a Christian friend stumbling repeatedly through the same mistakes while we do nothing to help him see his errors.

Better is open rebuke than love that is concealed.
(Proverbs 27:5 NAS)

Like apples of gold in settings of silver is a word spoken in right circumstances. *(Proverbs 25:11 NAS)*

In the culture of biblical days, hospitality was of extreme importance. Etiquette prescribed that one had to have fruit on hand with which to refresh weary travelers. Kitchilika trees produced an especially refreshing fruit which looked much like a cross between a grapefruit and an orange. The closest western biblical translators could come in description was "apples of gold," and the fruit would be served on a silver tray. This proverb is saying that a word spoken at the right time and in the right way refreshes hearts like kitchilika fruit refreshes weary travelers. We are to refresh one another's hearts in the unity and love of our Lord Christ Jesus.

🐑 *John* . . . We are to speak the wisdom we know and not hide it. Truth spoken in love is refreshment. We need to refresh one another by rebuking one another, but my own sin is that very seldom can I make myself do the rebuking. Why? Because I saw people in my childhood confronting each other in very harmful ways.

That didn't necessarily mean I feared I would do it in harmful ways myself, but my unforgiveness of those who rebuked others with harsh criticism locked me into a determination that I would not make the same mistake. Consequently, I make the opposite mistake of not issuing good and loving rebukes when I should.

Strangely, I have discovered that I can't get free of that until I repent of fleeing the role I am destined to play in my brother's life, causing him to fall because I failed to give him a word of loving rebuke.

In this way, love is made complete among us so that we will have confidence on the day of judgment, because in this world we are like him. There is no fear in love. But perfect love drives out fear, because fear has to do with punishment. The one who fears is not made perfect in love.   *(1 John 4:17)*

Blows and wounds cleanse away evil, and beatings purge the inmost being.   *(Proverbs 20:30)*

We should not fear that our rebukes, lovingly given, will bring hurt. Of course they may, but the value of the healing is greater.

Therefore we do not lose heart. Though outwardly we are wasting away, yet inwardly we are being renewed day by day. For our light and momentary troubles are achieving for us an eternal glory that far outweighs them all. So we fix our eyes not on what is seen, but on what is unseen. For what is seen is temporary, but what is unseen is eternal.
(2 Corinthians 4:16-18)

All of us need to receive blows that reach our inmost parts because that is the way we learn lessons and are cleansed.

We also need to understand the law of sowing and reaping. When we sow an evil deed, that sin accumulates toward heavier and heavier reaping until we repent. If a brother recognizes sin in us and rebukes us in the Lord, then we can repent, and the Lord will lift from us the consequences we are due and we will not be crushed. But if we are not rebuked, our sin will accumulate more and more dire reaping, until we reap the full harmful weight of it. Should we not then welcome the loving rebuke of a brother who cares enough to warn us of our errors, that we might repent before the crushing weight of full reaping comes?

> *Penalties are prepared for mockers, and beatings for the backs of fools.*   *(Proverbs 19:29)*

We must understand that it is love to rebuke. If we do not warn our brothers and sisters, they will reap heavier penalties and we will share the sin for withholding our love. Having the courage to speak a loving rebuke begins with our own repentance for wounding the Body if we stay silent.

6. If we fail to forgive each other, it makes us vulnerable to attack by Satan.

Satan wants to use any unforgivenesses he can find in our hearts as part of his scheme to create disharmony and destroy the unity of God's people. An unforgiving attitude not only separates individuals but it breaks down the unity that should be the strength of the Body of Christ. We must be on guard against giving him the opportunity to control our lives through the way he can nurture our hurts and bitternesses.

> *If anyone has caused grief, he has not so much grieved me as he has grieved all of you . . . If you forgive anyone, I also forgive him. And what I have forgiven, if there was anything to forgive—I have forgiven in the sight of Christ for your sake, in order that Satan might not outwit us. For we are not un-aware of his schemes.*   *(2 Corinthians 2:5-11)*

Satan wants to destroy the Church. His scheme is to encourage disharmony among believers in order to break down the unity of their obedience to Christ. The prayer of Jesus recorded in John 17 asked the Father to protect those who had come into unity with Him, and to bless their unity so that others might know the love of the Father through their witness. Jesus said:

*I in them and You in Me. May they be brought to complete
unity to let the world know that You sent me and have loved
them even as You have loved Me.*   *(John 17:23)*

Unity in the body of Christ validates Jesus before the world.
Disunity causes the world to disbelieve that Jesus is who He said
He is—sent by the Father. Satan uses any unforgivenesses he can
find to attack us in the vulnerability of our wounds. We play into
Satan's hands when through pride and self-righteous anger, we cut
others off, hold grudges, attempt to emotionally punish those who
may have wronged us, or refuse to allow the healing of God's grace
to be extended to others.

*In your anger do not sin. Do not let the sun go down while you
are still angry, and do not give the devil a foothold . . . Get rid
of all bitterness, rage and anger, brawling and slander, along
with every form of malice. Be kind and compassionate to one
another, forgiving each other, just as in Christ, God forgave
you.*   *(Ephesians 4:26-27, 31-32)*

**7. Hanging on to unforgiveness creates in us the necessity
to build and maintain a facade.**

Jesus wants us to be totally honest, transparent, believable and
consistent. He wants the transformation of our inner being to be so
complete that what we show to others is who we truly are. We
must be willing to be washed clean inside and out. Otherwise, we
are but a superficial reflection of God's love, filled with impurity
behind our facade.

Whenever we remain unforgiving, we become like the Pharisees
who demanded compliance with the letter of the law, yet held intolerance and self-righteousness within their hearts.

*Now then, you Pharisees clean the outside of the cup and dish,
but inside you are full of greed and wickedness. You foolish
people! Did not the One who made the outside make the inside
also?*   *(Luke 11:39-40)*

Both in action and in attitude we must be transparent, allowing God's love and grace to permeate our entire being. Purity within and without invites others to know us without reservation. Unforgiveness lodged in our heart creates a false, fleshly protective wall that separates who we really are from the image we project to the world.

♦ We don't want people to know our innermost thoughts and motivations so we erect barriers to keep others from getting too close.

♦ We don't invite others into fellowship with us for fear they'll see the truth of our family life.

♦ We avoid telling stories on ourselves because we have to maintain an image of having it all together.

♦ We are afraid to go to a counselor because we know we will be confronted and have to deal with issues that may be painful.

♦ We can't risk or be spontaneous because we have a need to keep everything under control.

♦ We can't adventure because we're insecure if asked to move outside our comfort zone and risk things we aren't sure will work.

♦ We don't trust others to love and accept us if they really knew who we are.

Building facades such as these to protect our unforgivenesses means that we are living a lie. That puts a terrific amount of stress on us—stress which will eventually take its toll in alienation from others and from God, breaking the unity of the kingdom. *We must not use the security of our own salvation experience to excuse that part of us which remains unregenerate.*

> *We love because He first loved us. If anyone says, "I love God," yet hates his brother, he is a liar. For anyone who does not love his brother, whom he has seen, cannot love God, whom he has not seen.* (1 John 4: 19-20)

> *If we claim to have fellowship with Him yet walk in the darkness, we lie and do not live by the truth. But if we walk in the*

*light, as He is in the light, we have fellowship with one an-
other, and the blood of Jesus, His Son, purifies us from all sin.*
(1 John 1: 6-7)

**8. Holding on to unforgiveness produces physical, emo-
tional, and spiritual exhaustion.**

We become exhausted trying to carry all of life's weight by ourselves, yet our pride and self-will compel us to stay in fleshly self-
control. Jesus invites us to give the load to Him. He promises to
relieve the burden, to give us rest and to be a gentle teacher.

*Come to Me, all you who are weary and burdened, and I will
give you rest. Take My yoke upon you and learn from Me, for
I am gentle and humble in heart, and you will find rest for
your souls. For My yoke is easy and My burden is light.*
(Matthew 11:28)

🍎 *John* . . . What is it that stops us? Is it that we do not trust
Him to be true to His word?. There have been times in my life when
I spent all my energies searching—first down one blind alley and
then another.

I got so tired, so completely exhausted that finally I said, *"Lord,
I can't make it. Even with Your grace and with Your Holy Spirit, if
it's up to me I can't make it. I am totally lost and depraved. There
is no way that I am going to be a viable person. I give up. I am
totally tired and exhausted. From now on I'm going to forget about
me and just live to bless people in Your Kingdom."*

Only when I got to that place did real freedom and joy come
into my life. I was no longer focusing on trying to get me straightened out. I focused my life on ministering to other people. I reck-
oned that my own enlightenment was not as important as God's call
to give myself to help others.

God still had, and has, more to straighten out in me. Inner
healing was and still is necessary. But now He had changed my focus and my motives. It was no longer that I would *use* inner healing
to get me straightened out, for my own selfish self-centered sake. I
determined to serve Him for His kingdom's purposes, forgetting
about me; and when He knew that my unhealed nature would harm

His kingdom and His purposes, then He would step in to heal my inner nature. I was now free from the quest for my own healing and left it up to God.

That was the repentance the Lord was waiting for. That was the turn around in my life, and it came nearly fifteen years after I was converted! From the time I repented of my own selfish search, my burden was lightened, my joy began to soar, and my pathway began to clear. All of life turned for the better because I was no longer trying to use God to straighten myself out. I determined to live for other people, for God's love of unity, and keep my eyes on His Kingdom.

What happens when we let Jesus restore unity through the joys of forgiveness?

If we are serious in our repentance and our desire to follow Jesus, we will be true to our faith and follow His commands. We will not play into the hands of the enemy. Rather, we will live out the vision and mission of our Lord. Jesus said:

> *The thief comes only to steal and kill and destroy; I have come that they may have life, and have it to the full [more abundantly].* *(John 10:10)*

1. When Jesus cleans us from the inside out, forgiveness transforms us.

Forgiveness changes our hardness of heart into compassion. We become consistently pure and transparent. Forgiveness makes life richer, more filled with love, more expansive, more spiritually alive, more abundantly satisfying. Although we may disagree with others, we appreciate the differences. We begin to value diversity. We learn to appreciate people for the way they provide balance for us—lifting, enriching, blessing, fulfilling—and yes, challenging and wounding us as well. We appreciate the ways differences, challenges, rebukes, and woundings drive us to perfection for Him.

Living in forgiveness means we are no longer threatened by others, nor do we feel accused. We get out of the business of competing and grow into the capacity to participate wholeheartedly in the joys of others and in what the Holy Spirit is doing in their lives. We rejoice more in what is happening with someone else than we do in what is happening with us.

Forgiveness allows us to let go of negative feelings and enter into a unity of fellowship with others so that everything that is joy and blessing for them is also our joy and blessing. Because of this attitude, we ourselves are refreshed and lifted up.

2. Those who live in forgiveness are given real spiritual authority.

Authority does not come from us. It comes from God and is based on God's Word, His Holy Spirit, His kingdom, and His authority.

> *Again Jesus said, "Peace be with you! As the Father has sent Me, I am sending you." And with that He breathed on them and said, "Receive the Holy Spirit. If you forgive anyone his sins, they are forgiven; if you do not forgive them, they are not forgiven."*   *(John 20: 21-23)*

We know through the authority given us by Christ that if we pronounce a forgiveness, it is going to happen. That authority is real because it has been given by God, and we know it because we have experienced it. Once we have experienced forgiveness in our own life, we know it can happen and we can be confident in God's power.

3. Living in forgiveness means we will come into rest and freedom.

The reason is obvious. Forgiveness allows us to escape the battle of trying to hold things together by ourselves, and it relieves the stress of trying to hide the inconsistencies in our life. When we trust the Lord, we give up everything to Him and come into a blessedness of rest.

You will keep in perfect peace him whose mind is steadfast, because he trusts in You.   *(Isaiah 26:3)*

Come to Me, all you who are weary and burdened, and I will give you rest. Take My yoke upon you and learn from Me, for I am gentle and humble in heart, and you will find rest for your souls. For My yoke is easy and My burden is light.   *(Matthew 11:28-29)*

There remains, therefore, a Sabbath rest for the people of God. For the one who has entered His rest has himself also rested from his works, as God did from His.   *(Hebrews 4:9-10 NAS)*

God commands a blessing where there is unity!

So I prophesied as I was commanded. And as I was prophesying, there was a noise, a rattling sound, and the bones came together, bone to bone. I looked, and tendons and flesh appeared on them and skin covered them, but there was no breath in them. Then He said to me, "Prophesy to the breath; prophesy, son of man, and say to it, This is what the sovereign Lord says: Come from the four winds, O breath, and breathe into these slain, so they may live." So I prophesied as He commanded me, and breath entered them; they came to life and stood up on their feet—a vast army.   *(Ezekiel 37:7-10)*

Most of us in the Body of Christ have not yet experienced the power of the Spirit of God that descended at Pentecost. As in Ezekiel 37, the Spirit of God has breathed upon us, stirring us from our spiritual death like the reassembly of scattered dry bones on a desert floor. But we have only risen as individuals.

In the awakening of our sense of forgiveness toward others, our dry bones have rattled together, so the Lord has caused us to begin to have tendons and flesh. But there is not yet any real vitality and power within us. We have not yet seen the fullness of Pentecost.

Peter and John walked up to a man lame from birth, who had never learned how to walk, whose muscles were atrophied. They did not even pray. Peter said, *"Look at us!"* And then said, *"I do not possess silver and gold, but what I do have I give to you: In the name of Jesus Christ the Nazarene—walk!" (Acts 3:4, 6)* The man not only walked, he leaped and ran! That's power! We pray and hope something happens—and are surprised if it does. They knew they had the power *resident within them*, and could transmit it.

In Ezekiel's vision, the Lord commanded him to prophesy to the "breath," that it might come from the four winds and bring life to those dry bones. That means to call for the Holy Spirit to come, to act in power upon and in us. At the second breathing of the Spirit, the bones came to life and stood up as a *vast army.*

The prophecy we must respond to now is for that second breathing to come which will make us a great army. Like the disciples of Jesus who were waiting in the upper room, we have been breathed on the first time and the Spirit of the Lord is within us. But the real power has yet to descend.

> *Again Jesus said, "Peace be with you! As the Father has sent Me, I am sending you." And with that He* **breathed on them and said, "Receive the Holy Spirit."**   *(John 20:21-22)*

Before Pentecost, the Holy Spirit was already with the disciples, just as the Spirit is with us, and the Spirit had already revealed many things to them. But Jesus counseled them to stay in Jerusalem and wait for that which he had promised them. In time the Spirit would descend and imbue them with *power*.

> *But you will receive* **power** *when the Holy Spirit comes on you; and you will be My witnesses in Jerusalem, and in all Judea and Samaria, and to the ends of the earth.*   *(Acts 1:8)*

What was the purpose of the delay? Why not receive that power from on high immediately? They had to be prepared by coming into unity. One hundred and twenty people spent ten days locked in an upper room, dealing with their issues. They sat down and started talking. They worked through their hassles and disagreements. They started confronting one another and speaking the truth. They discussed and selected who among them would take the place of Judas among the twelve. When they had talked it all out, prayed for one another and had forgiven each other, they came into corporateness. They achieved unity.

That was the ground of power the Holy Spirit needed. When they were all of one accord, the Holy Spirit was able to come and equip them in power to do the work of Christ in the world. Where there is unity, there God commands blessing.

Why don't we have fullness of power in our lives? Why do we lack power in our churches and in our denominations? It is because we have been living in our own little worlds, interested primarily in getting Jesus to bring us into personal salvation and to straighten out our own personal conflicts. We have almost no sense of the corporateness of our faith. We go about our own petty personal concerns unrepentant of how we may be contributing to tearing apart the fabric of the Body of Christ.

We don't have our eyes open to the Kingdom of God which is the central focus of what the Lord Jesus Christ came to establish! Since we haven't become corporate by forgiving one another, caring for one another, and praying for one another, the fullness of power through God's Holy Spirit has not been received.

This is why we need forgiveness. We haven't caught the vision of what we mean in Christ to each other. When we get that, and are really open to one another and share with one another in love, then the power will descend.

Our Heavenly Father,

We are so grateful that looking upon us You did not leave us in the isolation, loneliness, and despair which our sinfulness fully deserves. But rather You moved upon us to gather us up to Yourself. You moved upon us so that we might become one people, united in love through our Lord, Jesus Christ.

Lord, we confess that we have not really seen our oneness, and have not really discovered the corporateness to which You have called us. This is our sin. Not the only one, but certainly that which acts to block healthy relationships with others and to prevent the fullness of Your kingdom.

Lord, we want to understand forgiveness and corporateness and truly be the Body of Christ, doing Your work in the world. Help our spirits stay awake in Your Spirit and to be alert that we will hear and understand what You would give us each day.

Amen

Life Application:

Restoration of Christian Unity
Forgiveness at the Heart of God's Kingdom

1. Consider the statement on page 167: *"God is interested in more than just our personal salvation. He wants us to share in the restoration of unity throughout creation, fulfilling His purpose throughout the heavens."*

♦ Think about the areas where you influence people on a regular basis beyond your immediate family. Identify ways you can become more constructively involved to encourage unity in these broader issues of life.

2. If we are to be truly corporate, we must feel a linkage to all of our brothers and sisters and take responsibility for restoring unity where the sin of any (or all) has caused a separation.

♦ Identify several areas of disunity within the family of God for which you can express repentance for the sake of the entire Church.

♦ On behalf of the Church, ask for God's forgiveness for these corporate and personal sins.

3. Review the eight results of hanging on to unforgiveness listed on pages 172-186.

♦ Evaluate yourself to discover ways in which each of these situations applies to a relationship problem you currently face.

♦ Focus on one of these situations and repentantly confess to God your contribution to the problem and ask His forgiveness.

♦ What can you now do to remedy the situation with the person or persons involved?

4. For continuing application through the following weeks and months, make a list of every significant person in your life since birth.

♦ Write out details of how each of these persons impacted you both positively and negatively.

♦ Get in touch with any repressed grudges or even rage toward these persons.

♦ Make a choice to forgive each of them by name, even if they don't deserve it. Forgive each of them for the specific offenses committed against you.

♦ Pray for the Lord Jesus Christ to take the unforgiveness from you and put it to death on His cross.

Postlude

Daily thoughts for the journey toward forgiveness.

Quotations from this book and the accompanying Scripture references serve as a 31-day devotional guide to nourish you along your journey toward forgiveness.

১◆Day 1

What will I make of this day? Will I be a helpless victim choosing to live in bitterness, or a proactive affirmer of life, willing to forgive and to bless those who would harm me? Each moment is mine! No matter what my journey has been; no matter what nurturing or lack of nurturing I have experienced; no matter what pain and scars I bear—from this moment on, life is a choosing.

> *Therefore as God's chosen people, holy and dearly loved, clothe yourselves with compassion, kindness, humility, gentleness, and patience. Bear with each other and forgive whatever grievances you may have against one another. Forgive as the Lord forgave you. And over all these virtues put on love, which binds them all together in perfect unity.* (Colossians 3:12-14)

১◆Day 2

Sin is what isolates us from God and from one another. Unforgiveness preserves and calcifies the isolation, keeping us from seeking reconciliation and wholeness. Choosing forgiveness is an antidote to that poison of sin.

> *In your anger do not sin. Do not let the sun go down while you are still angry, and do not give the devil a foothold.*
> *(Ephesians 4:26)*

❧Day 3

If we are to be happy, healthy, and grow in relationships with others, forgiveness is not an option; it is a necessity. Choose this day, what you will do, and how you will respond to the hurts in your life.

> *And when you stand praying, if you hold anything against anyone, forgive him, so that your Father in heaven may forgive your sins.*
> *(Mark 11: 25-26)*

❧Day 4

God gives us the ability to make choices, but we must live with the results of our choosing. We can be stuck with unforgiveness forever and be miserable, or we can choose to forgive and enjoy the benefits of freedom forgiveness brings.

> *Make every effort to live in peace with all men and to be holy; without holiness no one will see the Lord. See to it that no one misses the grace of God and that no bitter root grows up to cause trouble and defile many.*   *(Hebrews 12:14-15)*

❧Day 5

The principle of sowing and reaping is one of God's absolute laws. If we sow unforgiveness, we will reap unforgiveness. If we sow forgiveness, we will reap forgiveness. Which will we choose?

> *Do not be deceived: God cannot be mocked. A man reaps what he sows. The one who sows to please his sinful nature will reap destruction; the one who sows to please the Spirit, from the Spirit will reap eternal life. Let us not become weary in doing good, for at the proper time we will reap a harvest if we do not give up. Therefore, as we have opportunity, let us do good to all people, especially those who belong to the family of believers.*   *(Galatians 6:7-10)*

❧Day 6

The process of forgiveness must begin with a simple act of choosing to begin the journey of forgiveness—of being willing to say, "I want to forgive."

> *May the Lord make your love increase and overflow for each other and for everyone else, just as ours does for you. May He strengthen your hearts so that you will be blameless and holy in the presence*

of our God and Father when the Lord Jesus comes with all His holy
ones.   *(1 Thessalonians 3:12-13)*

❧Day 7

To show true love toward others is to respect them enough to allow them to be accountable, particularly for the wounds they inflict
on other people. Love and forgiveness should not shield even
those we love the most from the consequences of their decisions.

> *Jesus said to His disciples: "Things that cause people to sin are*
> *bound to come, but woe to that person through whom they come. It*
> *would be better for him to be thrown into the sea with a millstone*
> *tied around his neck than for him to cause one of these little ones to*
> *sin. So watch yourselves. If your brother sins, rebuke him, and if he*
> *repents, forgive him. If he sins against you seven times in a day,*
> *and seven times comes back and says, I repent, forgive him."*
> *(Luke 17:1-4)*

❧Day 8

Forgiveness is not the same as pardoning. To pardon is to end all
judgment, to lift away all due reaping for sowing. God may pardon
if He so chooses. We are called and given authority only to forgive.

> *Seek the Lord while He may be found; call on Him while He is near.*
> *Let the wicked forsake his way and the evil man his thoughts. Let*
> *him turn to the Lord, and He will have mercy on him, and to our*
> *God, for he will freely pardon.*   *(Isaiah 55:6-7)*

❧Day 9

Those who struggle with forgiveness may say, "I have tried and
tried to forgive, and I just can't seem to get it done." If we think it
is up to us to accomplish forgiveness through our own striving, we
will never "get it done."

> *Therefore, if anyone is in Christ, he is a new creation; the old has*
> *gone, the new has come! All this is from God, who reconciled us to*
> *Himself in Christ, not counting men's sins against them. And He*
> *has committed to us the message of reconciliation. We are therefore*
> *Christ's ambassadors, as though God were making His appeal*
> *through us. We implore you on Christ's behalf: Be reconciled to*

God. God made Him who had no sin to be sin for us, so that in Him we might become the righteousness of God. (2 Corinthians 5:17-20)

≈•Day 10

Sometimes, in God's wisdom, He knows shortcuts won't be good for us; we'll have to take the long road of struggle and discipline, making ourselves obey when everything in us cries out to go the other way.

> *Therefore, my dear friends, as you have always obeyed—not only in my presence, but now much more in my absence—continue to work out your salvation with fear and trembling, for it is God who works in you to will and to act according to His good purpose.*
> *(Philippians 2:12-13)*

≈•Day 11

We must continually remind ourselves that the Lord has a work to do in us, and we had better clear the way by choosing to forgive.

> *I thank my God every time I remember you. In all my prayers for all of you, I always pray with joy because of your partnership in the Gospel from the first day until now, being confident of this, that He who began a good work in you will carry it on to completion until the day of Christ Jesus.*
> *(Philippians 1:3-6)*

≈•Day 12

I give up my right to be paid back for my loss by the one who has sinned against me—and in so doing, I declare my trust in God alone as my righteous judge.

> *Which of you, if his son asks for bread, would give him a stone? Or if he asks for a fish, would give him a snake? If you, then, though you are evil, know how to give good gifts to your children, how much more will your Father in heaven give good gifts to those who ask Him! So in everything, do to others what you would have them do to you, for this sums up the law and the prophets.*
> *(Matthew 7:9-12)*

≈Day 13

I ask Jesus, my Healer, to please release the Comforter to take my pain. It is too heavy and crippling to continue to carry, and I cannot heal myself.

> *Praise be to the God and Father of our Lord Jesus Christ, the Father of compassion and the God of all comfort, who comforts us in our troubles, so that we can comfort those in any trouble with the comfort we ourselves have received from God. For just as the sufferings of Christ flow into our lives, so also through Christ our comfort overflows.* (2 Corinthians 1:3-5)

≈Day 14

My choice to be vulnerable is my own and transparency is my own. No one can take them from me. They are mine to give and take back whenever I want. What freedom and release there is in for-giveness!

> *For you were once darkness, but now you are light in the Lord. Live as children of light. (For the fruit of the light consists in all good-ness, righteousness and truth) and find out what pleases the Lord. Have nothing to do with the fruitless deeds of darkness, but rather expose them. For it is shameful even to mention what the disobedi-ent do in secret. But everything exposed by the light becomes visi-ble, for it is light that makes everything visible. This is why it is said, "Wake up, O sleeper, rise from the dead, and Christ will shine on you."* (Ephesians 5:8-14)

≈Day 15

A life of unforgiveness is a life of bitterness and torment, a life open to demonic oppression, bondage to addictions and compulsive behaviors which seek to gratify the flesh in some hope of alleviating constant emotional stress. It is a life of unrest and violence—and really no kind of life at all.

> *Put to death therefore, whatever belongs to your earthly nature: sexual immorality, impurity, lust, evil desires and greed, which is idolatry. Because of these, the wrath of God is coming. You used to walk in these ways, in the life you once lived. But now you must rid yourselves of all such things as these: anger, rage, malice, slander, and filthy language from your lips.* (Colossians 3:5-8)

❧Day 16

Judging others to place blame serves only to deepen feelings of alienation and to keep us from seriously considering our own need for repentance. There is real hope only for those who are willing to cry out: "Oh Lord, have mercy upon me, for I am a sinner! Have mercy upon us, for we are all sinners!"

> *If we confess our sins, He is faithful and just and will forgive us our sins and purify us from all unrighteousness. If we claim we have not sinned, we make Him out to be a liar and His word has no place in our lives.*   *(1 John 1:9-10)*

❧Day 17

As Christians, we should recognize that unforgiveness is a sin issue which cannot be remedied through our striving. Without the power of Jesus, we can expect little relief. Forgiveness only gets done when it is taken to the cross.

> *At one time we, too, were foolish, disobedient, deceived and enslaved by all kinds of passions and pleasures. We lived in malice and envy, being hated and hating one another. But when the kindness and love of God our Savior appeared, He saved us, not because of righteous things we had done, but because of His mercy. He saved us by the washing and rebirth and renewal by the Holy Spirit, whom He poured out on us through Jesus Christ our Savior, so that, having been justified by His grace, we might become heirs having the hope of eternal life.*   *(Titus 3:3-7)*

❧Day 18

Irritants in life may not be worth elevating to a major issue, but they must be dealt with on some level rather than just stuffing them down inside.

> *When I kept silent, my bones washed away through my groaning all day long. For day and night Your hand was heavy upon me; my strength was sapped as in the heat of summer. Then I acknowledged my sin to You and did not cover up my iniquity. I said, "I will confess my transgressions to the Lord"—and You forgave the guilt of my sin.*   *(Psalm 32:3-5)*

❧Day 19

Giving our unforgiveness to the Lord requires that we trust in the Lord Jesus Christ as Savior. We must accept Him as the Son of God who has authority and power to forgive sins, to overcome death, and to make us into new beings. We must come to Him repentantly so that we become malleable spirits in whom Jesus can work.

Therefore, there is now no condemnation for those who are in Christ Jesus, because through Christ Jesus the law of the Spirit of life set me free from the law of sin and death. For what the law was powerless to do in that it was weakened by the sinful nature, God did by sending His own Son in the likeness of sinful man to be a sin offering. And so He condemned sin in sinful man, in order that the righteous requirements of the law might be fully met in us, who do not live according to the sinful nature but according to the Spirit.

(Romans 8:1-4)

❧Day 20

True forgiveness is demonstrated in our willingness to pray for and facilitate good things happening in the life of the one who has hurt us. Without that, we miss the point of our forgiveness and fall short of the blessing of grace which God has for us.

Never be lacking in zeal, but keep your spiritual fervor, serving the Lord. Be joyful in hope, patient in affliction, faithful in prayer. Share with God's people who are in need. Practice hospitality. Bless those who persecute you; bless and do not curse. Rejoice with those who rejoice; mourn with those who mourn. Live in harmony with one another.

(Romans 12:11-16)

❧Day 21

We cannot experience the anguish of betrayal and the pain of alienation and remain the same persons we were. Nor can we expect the other person to remain unchanged. Reconciliation brings with it new perimeters of knowledge, understanding, and feelings. Forgiveness may heal anger and bitterness, but realistically may fall short of reconciliation or even of establishing a friendly relationship.

So then, those who suffer according to God's will should commit themselves to their faithful Creator and continue to do good.

(1 Peter 4:19)

ᐅ Day 22

In the name of honesty and in an attempt to defuse our angers, we can go around spilling all that is in our hearts, thinking that speaking feelings is the same as dealing with them. But without repentance and willingness to give over angers to Jesus to be put to death on the cross, what we are actually doing is continually rehearsing our negative feelings and destroying the fabric of unity wherever we go.

> *With the tongue we praise our Lord and Father, and with it we curse men, who have been made in God's likeness. Out of the same mouth come praise and cursing. My brothers, this should not be.*
> *(James 3:9-10)*

ᐅ Day 23

Jesus accomplishes forgiveness in us, but we must first repentantly confess our feelings and seek to forgive as a daily moment-by-moment discipline. This must be practiced repeatedly, continuously, so that our hearts are softened and our negative feelings become malleable to change. This opens us to receive the grace of Jesus Christ and leads to release and healing.

> *Get rid of all bitterness, rage and anger, brawling and slander, along with every form of malice. Be kind and compassionate to one another, forgiving each other, just as in Christ God forgave you*
> *(Ephesians 4:31-32)*

ᐅ Day 24

Individual hurts may seem like tiny barbs we can pass off by saying they don't really bother us. But when we get a whole pin cushion full of needles, we start experiencing emotional and physical pain and discomfort that makes life miserable. The most healthy thing we can do is honestly admit feelings and seek a way to constructively remove those painful barbs through forgiveness.

> *Be still before the Lord and wait patiently for Him; do not fret when men succeed in their ways, when they carry out their wicked schemes. Refrain from anger and turn from wrath; do not fret—it leads only to evil.*   *(Psalm 37:7-8)*

¿⚬Day 25

We can't expect Christ to intervene when we pray confessing another person's sin. We must confess our own sin and be willing to do whatever is necessary to set things straight.

> *And the prayer offered in faith will make the sick person well; the Lord will raise him up. If he has sinned, he will be forgiven. Therefore confess your sins to each other and pray for each other so that you may be healed. The prayer of a righteous man is powerful and effective.* (James 5:15-16)

¿⚬Day 26

To have reverence for Christ means to allow Him access within us to accomplish effectively everything for which He died on the cross. That means we need to submit to Him all of our feelings, our past, our present, our daily irritations, our demanding attitudes, our manipulations, and our unforgivenesses.

> *For we do not have a high priest who is unable to sympathize with our weaknesses, but we have one who has been tempted in every way, just as we are—yet was without sin. Let us then approach the throne of grace with confidence, so that we may receive mercy and find grace to help us in our time of need.* (Hebrews 4:15-16)

¿⚬Day 27

Our angers and unforgivenesses are our own and grow out of our need to control. However, God can use every circumstance of life to bring blessing to us and to write wisdom in our hearts if we respond according to His will.

> *And we know that God causes all things to work together for good to those who love God, to those who are called according to his purpose.* (Romans 8:28 NAS)

❧Day 28

We play into Satan's hands when through pride and self-righteous anger, we cut others off, hold grudges, attempt to emotionally punish those who may have wronged us, or refuse to allow the healing of God's grace to be extended to others.

> *Do nothing out of selfish ambition or vain conceit, but in humility consider others better than yourselves. Each of you should look not only to your own interests, but also to the interests of others.*
> *(Philippians 2:3-4)*

❧Day 29

Forgiveness allows us to escape the battle of trying to hold everything together by ourselves, and it relieves the stress of trying to hide the inconsistencies in our lives. When we trust the Lord, we give everything up to Him and come into a blessedness of rest.

> *Come to Me, all you who are weary and burdened, and I will give you rest. Take My yoke upon you and learn from Me, for I am gentle and humble in heart, and you will find rest for your souls. For My yoke is easy and My burden is light.* *(Matthew 11:28-29)*

❧Day 30

Forgiveness allows us to let go of the negative feelings and enter into a unity of fellowship with others so that everything that is joy and blessing for them is also our joy and blessing. Because of this attitude, we ourselves are refreshed and lifted up.

> *Love is patient, love is kind. It does not envy, it does not boast, it is not proud. It is not rude, it is not self-seeking, it is not easily angered, it keeps no record of wrongs. Love does not delight in evil but rejoices with the truth. It always protects, always trusts, always hopes, always perseveres.* *(1 Corinthians 13:4-6)*

≈⊌Day 31

Forgiveness changes our hardness of heart into compassion. For-giveness makes life richer, more filled with love, more expansive, more spiritually alive, more abundantly satisfying. Although we may disagree with others, we learn to appreciate people for the way they provide balance for us—lifting, enriching, blessing, fulfill-ing—and challenging and wounding us as well. We appreciate the way differences, challenges, rebukes and woundings drive us to perfection for the Lord.

> *Therefore, since we have been justified through faith, we have peace with God through our Lord Jesus Christ, through whom we have gained access by faith into this grace in which we now stand. And we rejoice in the hope of the glory of God. Not only so, but we also rejoice in our sufferings, because we know that suffer-ing produces perseverance; perseverance, character; and charac-ter, hope. And hope does not disappoint us, because God has poured out His love into our hearts by the Holy Spirit, whom He has given us.* (Romans 5:1-5)

Materials available through Elijah House

Elijah House, Inc.
S. 1000 Richards Rd. Post Falls, ID 83854 Phone (208) 773-1645

Books by John and Paula Sandford
The Elijah Task
Restoring the Christian Family
The Transformation of the Inner Man
Healing the Wounded Spirit

by John & Paula Sandford and Lee Bowman
Waking the Slumbering Spirit
Choosing Forgiveness

by John Sandford
Why Some Christians Commit Adultery

by Paula Sandford
Healing Victims of Sexual Abuse
Healing Women's Emotions

by John Sandford and Loren Sandford
The Renewal of the Mind

by John Sandford and Mark Sandford
Deliverance and Inner Healing

by Loren Sandford
Burnout: Renewal in the Wildernesss

By Howard Olsen
Wounded Warriors Chosen Lives: Healing for Vietnam Veterans

by Charles Wade, Lee and Carol Bowman
The Jesus Principle: Building Churches in the Likeness of Christ

Numerous audio and video tapes
are also available. Write for a catalog or
*visit the Elijah House web site **www.elijahhouse.org***

Acknowledgements

Special thanks to Carol Ricks Bowman for her wisdom and creative ideas in developing and organizing material for this book, and for her role as a wonderfully supportive wife, counselor, consultant, critic, and first-line proof-reader.

Charlie Finck, Howard Olsen, and Paul Haglin have all made wonderful contributions to this book by sharing their testimonies of spiritual pilgrimage and forgiveness. Their honesty and vulnerability through self-revelation are greatly appreciated.

Dick and Judy French have been good friends and colleagues in ministry. We appreciate their examples of forgiveness put into action, shared from counseling experiences and from their own lives.

Thanks also to Judy Prather, friend and publications staff member at Baylor University, for her extraordinary ability as proof-reader and stylist.

For quantity discounts on the purchase of
Waking the Slumbering Spirit,
Choosing Forgiveness,
Wounded Warriors Chosen Lives,
The Jesus Principle
contact the publisher:

Clear Stream Publishing
P.O. Box 122128 Arlington, TX 76012
(817) 265-2766 Fax (817) 861-0703
www.clear-stream.com